Sam K Sloan

10/20/89

▲

FROM
COACH
TO
COACH

REAL WORLD WISDOM FROM THE
ATHLETIC INDUSTRY'S FINEST

by SAM SHRIVER

FOREWORD by KENNETH BLANCHARD

Fulcourt Press

Escondido, CA

FROM COACH TO COACH

Library of Congress Catolog Card Number: 88-83038

ISBN 0-922192-00-6

Printed in the United States of America
First Edition

Book design by Greg High

You may obtain additional copies of this book directly from the publisher by contacting 1-800-433-3255, in California dial 619-747-8472.

Information regarding seminars should be directed to Performance IMPACT, Inc. at 619-747-8309.

◆ Dedication ◆

To
"Big E" and "The Duke"

. . . take a deep seat
and
a long rein.

“ Foreword **”**

I'll never forget when I was about five years old coming home and saying to my dad, "You know, I saw a bunch of the big kids down the street playing some game where they throw a ball at a basket. It's got a net and it looks like fun." He told me that was "basketball." The next Christmas Eve I remember being awakened and hearing all this noise downstairs. It was my father and one of his friends playing basketball in our basement. My big surprise for Christmas was that he had put up a basket for me. That was the beginning of my love for the fabulous game of basketball.

I have known Sam Shriver for almost a decade. When I first heard about him, I heard he was a great ball player. I also heard he was a great teacher. I knew him first as a trainer with a competitive training company and have now come to know him as a friend and colleague. I have seen Sam grow in his knowledge and skill. I'd say he's one of our industry's brightest young stars.

I'm very pleased that he has found a way to combine the two loves of his life . . . sports and management training, into the "From Coach To Coach" project. As you will see . . . there are many useful parallels between the two.

"From Coach To Coach" captures the insight of some of the top people in the game of basketball . . . people who have really been heroes of mine over the years like Jerry West, K.C. Jones and others. The book takes what these individuals have learned from working with and through others in the game of basketball at a variety of different levels and suggests techniques that can be applied to line management in other industries.

Sam's "Pyramid of Influence" details management's most important behind the scenes activities. Things like honesty, for example. I can't begin to emphasize how important that trait is. In fact, a recent study showed that when people were asked to describe the characteristics of a leader that they would follow, the primary criteria that 75% of the respondents identified as crucial was personal integrity.

The Pyramid also includes a discussion on Ego. My experience with managers is that the best are usually the ones that have their egos under control. Norman Vincent Peale and I talk about pride in our recent book, "The Power of Ethical Management." Managers who have trouble . . . and cause trouble . . . in organizations are often ones who don't feel good about themselves and try to overcompensate by controlling, evaluating and judging those around them.

These are just two of the primary arenas that "From Coach To Coach" covers. I'm convinced that the message found on the following pages will be powerful for you in your everyday life. Enjoy this book . . . its insight is easy to comprehend . . . and, when it comes right down to it, even easier to apply.

Kenneth H. Blanchard, Ph.D.
Co-author, "The One Minute Manager"

● Acknowledgements ●

One thing you quickly come to grips with when undertaking a project of this magnitude is the importance of the people around you. Some of them provide useful, structural comments about your manuscript; others re-charge your confidence coefficient when you're about ready to throw in the towel; still others find time to do "whatever it takes" to meet "an undoable" deadline or re-work a chapter draft for the fifteenth time. The following pages are intended to acknowledge the contributions of some very special people for their efforts on my behalf.

- Simply stated, this project never would have left the starting blocks if it weren't for the effort and vision of Greg Newell. His creative input early on, as well as his consistent follow-up with the celebrity talent after things got underway, helped transform an idea into 225 tangible pages.

- Special thanks to Dr. Freida Brown for her diligent research. "Freida's Facts" contributed significantly to the development of Chapters 1-5 and her focused input was a welcome addition throughout.

- Barbara Smits of Performance IMPACT, Inc. painstakingly typed, corrected, re-typed and re-corrected every word of this manuscript without a single word of complaint . . . (a single word that I could repeat in writing anyway). Thanks, Barb, . . . now get back to work!!

- To Rick Tate for his insight and input. Rick is the first person I ever heard talk about "core management behaviors" which is the central theme of Chapters 1-5.

- Greg High is responsible for all the graphics, cartoons and illustra-tions. If you really like them . . . give me a call at (800) 433-3255. If you find yourself repulsed by the artwork . . . please call Greg collect at home.

- Dick Ruhe and Charlie Ohlsson, full partners in Performance IMPACT, Inc., are also to be publicly thanked for dedicating their resources to this project.

- Right along side of Greg Newell in the task of securing celebrity talent was a fellow by the name of Roger Morningstar. Roger is an executive with Converse, Inc. and was responsible for putting Greg and I in contact with K.C. Jones, Doug Collins and Pat Head Summitt. Besides all that, Roger is one of the most hard working, down to earth, personable folks I've ever met. It was simply a pleasure to get to know him while we had the opportuunity to work together.

- Special thanks to Pete Newell, Jerry West, Claire Rothman, Wayne Embry, K.C. Jones, Doug Collins and Pat Head Summitt. Every one of them was a class act that legitimately practiced what I'm about to preach. It was a pleasure to work together and an honor to associate my name with their accomplishments.

- To Dana Pagett and the Rancho Santiago Dons as well as Greg Anton and the crew at Multiimage Productions who graciously volunteered to be photographed for the jacket.

- To Marianne Campbell for her editing expertise, critical evaluation and other valuable inputs.

- To Bill McHenry, Peter DiNicola and Tim Leahy for their thoughtful insight, constructive criticism and tenured friendship.

- To my parents, Van and Keith Shriver, for their relentless support throughout the years. I will consider myself very successful in life if their grandchildren think as much of me when they are my age as I do of them.

- To my wife, Maureen, for the strength, the encouragement, the support and the personal effort she has given to make this project a real product . . . Thank you!

■ *Special Acknowledgements* ■
Pete Newell and Ken Blanchard

I'd like to pay special tribute to two people, Pete Newell and Ken Blanchard. Realistically, either one of them could have stopped this project before it ever got started.

Mr. Newell took the first risk. He agreed to let me film his interview and use excerpts of it as a promotional tool with other celebrity talent. A Pete Newell endorsement within the Athletic Industry is a lot like Lee Iacocca putting his name behind your new car design in the automotive community . . . people feel almost compelled to let you in the door and hear what you have to say.

Interviews in hand, there was still the formidable challenge of turning an idea into a book. Ken Blanchard went well out of his way to offer advice, assistance and constructive criticism. He let me know point blank when he thought I was off target, but always presented his advice in a manner that communicated "stay with it," "I think you've got something here," "see this thing through."

Thanks to both of you for your support.

▼ CONTENTS ▼

INTRODUCTION   **1**

Chapter ONE – **HONESTY**   27

Chapter TWO – **WORK ETHIC**   61

Chapter THREE – **EGO**   97

Chapter FOUR – **WINNING & LOSING**   137

Chapter FIVE – **VISION**   167

Chapter SIX – **STYLE**   193

▲ INTRODUCTION▲

▲ INTRODUCTION ▲

First and foremost, thanks for taking the time to crack this cover and investigate its contents. I'm sure you could be doing a lot of other things right now, so your interest is much appreciated.

My intentions up front are to accomplish the following:

1) Give you a little background on this project.

2) Give you an overview of the concepts that will be presented in the next six chapters.

3) Introduce you to the seven coaches and managers that have consented to publicize their experience and insight on the enclosed pages.

Here goes.

The Background

▼ I guess I would have to say that I fall into that faction of the population that strongly believes athletic competition is a very positive element of our society. The thrill of victory . . . the agony of defeat . . . I'm into that stuff . . . and I think you can learn a lot about life by putting a ball through a basket, slapping a puck into a net, etc.

Admittedly, I shake my head in amazement every time a 25 year old "phenom" signs a no cut contract at ten times the annual salary of the President of the United States. Somehow, that always seems a tad ridiculous no matter how you shake it out.

Periodically, I also find myself devastated by the publicized accounts of prominent athletes using drugs . . . and wonder what effect that might have on my kids who will soon be old enough to actively idolize their favorite modern day gladiators.

Along the same lines, it disgusts me to think about the cheating that takes place in the athletic industry. The shortsightedness of those that blatantly disregard common sense ethical boundaries is simply beyond belief.

In open and honest acknowledgment of those unfortunate dynamics, few days of my professional life pass when I don't make some kind of positive use out of my personal experience in athletics, and actively create "then" and "now" scenarios about things like PREPARATION . . . PERFORMANCE . . . and POST EVENT ANALYSIS.

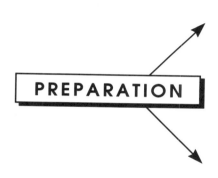

THEN:

Hell week . . . conditioning drills . . . weight room . . . bench jumps . . . suicides . . . stadium steps . . . jump ropes . . . offense . . . defense . . . press . . . game plan . . . walk through . . . pregame meal.

NOW:

Literature search . . . corporate report . . . phone calls . . . correspondence . . . projections . . . best case . . . worst case . . . initial position . . . fall back position . . . dry run . . . airline reservation.

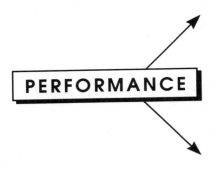

THEN:

Game uniform . . . cheerleaders . . .
packed house . . ."let's take it to
'em" . . . bad call!! . . . big break!!
. . . confidence . . . insecurity . . .
noise . . . tension . . . great win . . .
tough loss.

PERFORMANCE

NOW:

Dress for success . . . secretaries
. . . crowded room . . . "ok, let's
get started" . . . "so far so good"
. . . tough objection . . . great
comeback . . . order time . . .
tension . . . "we got the business"
. . . "they went with somebody
else".

THEN:

Exhausted . . . hot shower . . .
whirlpool . . . head high . . . head
low . . . high five . . . pat on the
back . . . "I still can't believe we
won". . . "We never should have
lost that one" . . . practice tomorrow . . . stat sheet . . . bus ride.

NOW:

Drained . . . phone calls . . . walking
on air . . . down in the dumps . . .
Party!! . . . "I just want to be alone
for awhile". . . bonus . . . wasted
effort . . . 22% ahead of plan . . .
16% behind . . . cold calls tomorrow . . .
expense report . . . plane ride.

This "analogy" process may or may not be applicable to your past and present . . . but at the very least I thought it might provide an explanation of the driving force behind the pages that follow. These pages will attempt to draw similar parallels between the world of athletics and the world of industry.

From my vantage point, coaches and front office executives in prime time athletics are among the most highly scrutinized, second guessed managers in existence. For example:

- Twenty million households had the opportunity to watch live and in color as Tommy Lasorda, long time manager of the Los Angeles Dodgers, weighed the pros and cons of each potential pitching change in the 1988 World Series.

- Eighteen million households, (in the United States alone), watched in angered disbelief as Anthony Hembrick, a 165 pound boxer on the United States Olympic team, forfeited his second round bout in Seoul because his managers had misread the schedule.

- Thousands of baseball fans across the country are amused at least once a year as George Steinbrenner, owner of the New York Yankees, plays revolving doors with his "on-field generals."

- Writers, radio broadcasters and tele-vision announcers alike interrogate "big league" coaches and managers every day of every season . . . then publicize objective . . . (and some-times subjective), accounts of those interrogations for public perusal.

- Won-loss percentages are also a mat-ter of public record . . . and if a high priced "bonus baby" is disgruntled with his lack of playing time, media representatives literally stand in line to play "point . . . counter point," (and do all they can to add fuel to the fire of controversy).

Without question, the world of the prime time coach is significantly impacted by a variety of unique high profile dynamics. By the same token, there is dramatic similarity between the task of managing a team of athletes . . . and the task of managing a sales district, a production department or a research project. For instance:

- All of the above are responsible for end results . . . whether that's a win-ning percentage above .500, a sales force that meets quota, or a produc-tion department that delivers on sched-ule and under budget.

- Coaches in all industries also have the responsibility to select talent and develop their followers' potential to the fullest. If a member of the team isn't performing up to standard . . . the coach/manager has to find out why . . . and then proceed to unleash a variety of corrective measures.

- Most managers, regardless of their profession, have encountered followers blessed with truckloads of God-given natural talent . . . but very little desire to put that talent to use.

- On the flip side of that coin, most managers have also experienced the frustration of having to deal with enthusiastic, "work horse" like employees that have little or no task specific skill.

The popularity of the industry is the variable . . . the issues associated with influence are relatively constant.

As such, I sat down with seven well respected representatives of the coaching profession. Some were "courtside" first level supervisors . . . and some were front office "behind the scenes" managers. All were time tested winners with impeccable reputations. Their records as players, coaches and managers literally speak for themselves.

The Coaches

● PETE NEWELL ●
Current Occupation: Consultant for the
Cleveland Cavaliers

Pete Newell

● CAREER HIGHLIGHTS ●

— Member Basketball Hall of Fame
— Coach of N.I.T. Champion USF
  DONS, 1949
— Coach of NCAA Champion California
  Bears, 1959
— Coach of United States Olympic
  Gold Medal Team, 1960
— Received Metropolitan Basketball
  Award for outstanding achievement
  in basketball, 1965
— General Manager of the Los Angeles
  Lakers, 1972-1976
— Overall Coaching Record: 234-123

● PAT HEAD SUMMITT ●

Current Occupation: Head Coach Women's Basketball
at the University of Tennessee

Pat Head Summitt

● CAREER HIGHLIGHTS ●

— Co-captain United States Olympic
  Silver Medal Team, 1976
— Coach of United States Olympic
  Gold Medal Team, 1984
— Coach of NCAA Champion
  Tennessee Volunteers, 1987
— Naismith College Coach of the Year,
  1987
— Led University of Tennessee Volun-
  teers to the Final Four in eight of
  the last eleven seasons
— Overall Coaching Record: 413-109

● K.C. JONES ●

Current Occupation: Boston Celtics Vice President
of Operations

K.C. Jones

● CAREER HIGHLIGHTS ●

— **Member of NCAA Champion USF
   DONS, 1955-56**
— **Member of United States Olympic
   Gold Medal Team, 1956**
— **Member of eight World Champion
   Boston Celtic teams, 1959-1966**
— **Coach of two World Champion
   Boston Celtic teams, 1984, 1986**
— **Only NBA coach to have 60 plus
   win seasons with two teams**
— **Overall Coaching Record: 463-193**

● CLAIRE ROTHMAN ●

Current Occupation: President, California FORUM

Claire Rothman

● CAREER HIGHLIGHTS ●

— Promoted to Business Manager of The Spectrum in Philadelphia, 1967
— Facility Manager of the Year **Billboard**, 1976, '79, '80, '81, '82
— The Forum named Facility of the Year **Billboard**, 1978
— Named one of the "Ten Women of the Decade" by Women in Business, 1984
— Woman of the Year Benefactor's Award **City of Hope**, 1986

● WAYNE EMBRY ●

Current Occupation:Vice President and General
Manager, Cleveland Cavaliers

Wayne Embry

● CAREER HIGHLIGHTS ●

— **Captain University of Miami (Ohio)
basketball team, 1956-58**
— **Captain of Cincinnati Royals
basketball team, 1962-66**
— **Member World Champion Boston
Celtics, 1968**
— **Named to the NBA All-Star team
5 times**
— **Named Vice President and General
Manager of the Milwaukee Bucks,
1972. (The first Black ever named
to a front office position in the NBA.)**
— **Named Vice President and General
Manager of the Cleveland Cavaliers,
1986**

● DOUG COLLINS ●

Current Occupation: Head Coach of the Chicago Bulls

Doug Collins

● CAREER HIGHLIGHTS ●

— **First Team Consensus All American from Illinois State, 1973**
— **Member of United States Olympic Silver Medal Team, 1972**
— **First player picked in the 1973 NBA draft**
— **Named Head Coach of the Chicago Bulls at the age of 34**
— **Led Bulls to a 50-32 record in 1987-88, their best since 1973**
— **Overall Coaching Record: 94-76**

● JERRY WEST ●

Current Occupation: General Manager of the
Los Angeles Lakers

Jerry West

● CAREER HIGHLIGHTS ●

— Co-captain of the United States
   Olympic Gold Medal Team, 1960
— Selected First Team All NBA
   10 times in a 14 year career
— Scored 25,194 points, sixth highest
   in NBA history
— Member of the 1971-72 World
   Championship Los Angeles
   Lakers
— General Manager of a World Cham-
   pionship team in three of his six
   years as a GM
— Overall Coaching Record: 145-101

"Basketball personalities" were chosen to interview for a number of reasons. Primarily:

- The numbers seem most compatible with the "span of control" most managers find themselves involved with in other industries (approximately 10-12).

- It's a team game played by a collection of individuals.

- Basketball coaches are not afforded the luxury of developing or relying on "specialists." For the most part, there are no "designated hitters . . . relief pitchers . . . goal line defenses or short yardage offenses." The five players on the court pretty much have to get it done on their own. This also seemed much more consistent with the situations faced by managers in other industries.

- (I like the game.)

To insure a positive mix of perspective with those that consented to provide input, it was important to have not only the courtside vantage point . . . but also the executive and administrative view as well. For example, Claire Rothman, President of The California Forum, has never played or coached in a major college or N.B.A. basketball game. Yet her behind the scenes coordination and logistic wizardry make it possible for the Lakers to thrive as one of the all time best "bottom line" franchises in N.B.A. history.

The graphic below attempts to locate each of the inter-viewees on a makeshift, organizational chart. Their comments should be taken with their "coaching" histories, as well as their current perspectives, in mind.

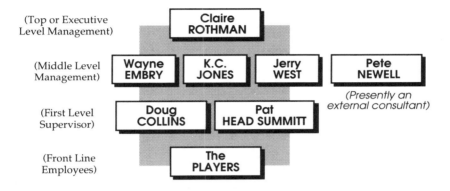

The Concept

▼ The initial intent of the interviews was to gain tactical advice. How do you motivate?? How do you lead others?? How do you discipline?? How do you reward?? What's the answer in the back of the book on being a successful coach??

Strangely enough, those interviewed spent precious little time talking about what they <u>did</u> to others . . . and the overwhelming majority of the time expounding on what they expected from themselves. They talked about holding themselves accountable for making ethical decisions . . . consistent and sometimes excessive work standards . . . keeping their egos in check . . . maximizing their team's potential . . . and keeping an eye on the future.

They talked about "simple" things . . . simple things that they did every day. One quote by Coach Pete Newell seemed to encapsulate the essence of every interview:

❝ *You know, Sam . . . there are two schools of thought in coaching. The school of "Surprise and Change" and the school of "Simplicity and Execution." Now in my fifty some odd years in this business, the great coaches . . . the great leaders . . . and for that matter the most successful programs, have been the "Simplicity and Executions." They don't do a lot of things, but they do them very well. They have no secrets . . . very few "gimmicks." They beat you through hard work, dedication and preparation.* ❞

Pete Newell

The following pages will present a "Pyramid of Influence" based on that very sage advice. The pyramid is made up of six topic areas for your consideration. These topic areas, in order of priority and presentation, are:

- **HONESTY**

- **WORK ETHIC**

- **EGO**

- **WINNING AND LOSING**

- **VISION**

- **STYLE**

CHAPTER 1 – HONESTY:

When it comes to influencing others, trust is everything. Whether it's your kids, your friends, your acquaintances at church or your front line employees . . . if they don't perceive you as honest, ethical and "up front" . . . your potential to point them in a desired direction is significantly reduced.

You also don't exactly have to be a brain surgeon these days to figure out that we are in the middle of a first rate ethical crisis in this country. Pick up today's paper . . . turn to any section you want . . . you'll find a current example in less than 60 seconds. Chapter 1 investigates this ethical impasse as well as the "perceptional" issues associated with determining what's ethical and what isn't. The chapter also offers "self help" ethical guidelines from those interviewed.

CHAPTER 2 – WORK ETHIC:

Two primary issues with work ethic:

- Those that don't do enough

- Those that do way too much

Again, critical self evaluation is the key. It's easy to see lack of effort in someone else . . . but how about yourself?? What could you be doing to increase your own level of competence? How might that increased level of competence assist you in your efforts to influence others?

On the flip side of the coin, what if you're putting in too much effort? . . . Haven't seen your kids in God knows how long . . . can't remember the last time you used a vacation day to just mess around with friends or family . . . the job has become "all encompassing" . . . what do you do then?

Chapter 2 offers advice on seeking some semblance of balance in your professional and personal life.

CHAPTER 3 – EGO:

What do people really want from their jobs? Why do they work in the first place? What about that faction of the population that's driven by self- esteem and pride in their work . . . how do you go about positioning yourself to influence that crew? What do you have to give up if you have people like that working for you??

In many cases, it's control . . . control of the day-to-day operation . . . control of the recognition for a job well done . . . control of the decision making process.

What's in it for you if you do? How do you go about it? These questions and others are addressed in Chapter 3.

CHAPTER 4 – WINNING AND LOSING:

Everybody wants to win . . . that's why you compete in the first place. No pain . . . no gain . . . no guts . . . no glory. But what happens when you become consumed by winning? Lose sight of reality? Can't take a short-term hit for a long-term benefit? In many cases, the answer is tragedy.

On the other hand, what about losing? How can losing be put into perspective? Used as a positive experience or a springboard for future success?

Chapter 4 shares the personal winning and losing experiences of seven folks who've done a lot of both and offers guidelines on putting individual outcomes into perspective.

CHAPTER 5 – VISION:

It's well documented that truly successful managers and coaches are forward thinking people. They see the future and position themselves and those around them to take advantage of it.

But seeing the future is more than sitting in your office with your feet up on your desk looking out a window. It's developing an in-depth appreciation of the past and a working knowledge of the present so you may influence the future.

Again, Chapter 5 relies on the input of the canvassed talent to provide some real world "how to's" in the arena of seeing the future.

CHAPTER 6 – STYLE:

As advertised, the first five chapters deal with internal issues. Self evaluation. When it comes right down to it, the things <u>you</u> control such as:

- Your ethical barometer

- The amount of effort you put . . . (or don't put), into a given task

- Your ego involvement in your team's success

- Your reaction and perspective on individual wins and losses

- Your ability to position yourself to predict future trends.

I would argue that if you have those five things going for you . . . you will be a very successful coach.

That notwithstanding, the "panel of experts" did offer some first rate "face-to-face" advice. Chapter 6 is an organized potpourri of "how to's" for one-on-one as well as one-on-group leadership situations.

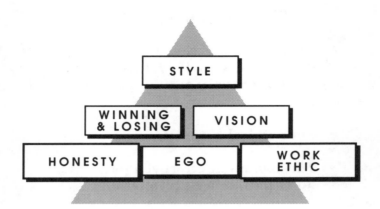

So there you have it . . . the Pyramid of Influence. The real world wisdom of some of the athletic industry's finest. I can only hope that you take as much from reading these pages as I have from having the opportunity to write them.

▲ HONESTY ▲

CHAPTER 1

▲ HONESTY ▲

Scenario 1

(A disillusioned department head shares future plans with a
confidant.)

*It was like a knife going through my heart. I simply couldn't
believe it. I stood there with the phone riveted to my ear, trying to
act like I was in control while the emptiness spread.*

*That promotion was in the bag! Joe gave me his word just last
week that he was going to support me 100%. Now, I hear from a
mutual acquaintance that he's bringing in somebody from Michigan . . . that the whole thing has already been finalized . . . and he
didn't even have the guts to tell me . . . that's just great.*

*Well, I can tell you this much . . . I'm not going to take this
lying down. Joe is playing "power broker" with the wrong person.
I don't know how and I don't know when, but you can bet on the
fact that he's going to regret this . . . big time!*

▲ hon•es•ty:
    **fairness and straightforwardness of conduct;
integrity; adherence to the facts; sincerity; up-
rightness of character or action; a refusal to
lie, steal, or deceive in any way.**

Overview

▼ Nobody likes to be lied to, yet people can justify it for a myriad of "good reasons." This chapter will focus on the issue of telling the truth, of honesty, of making ethical decisions in your personal and professional lives. It will focus on the importance of honesty when you are given the responsibility of influencing others.

This chapter will operate on the principle of the inverted pyramid. Initially we'll take a look at "The Facts" relevant to our present day ethical environment. We will then explore some of "The Costs" associated with ethical issues, "The Rationale" for dishonesty and/or unethical decision making and finally "The Choice" each of us has when dealing with others we have the opportunity to influence.

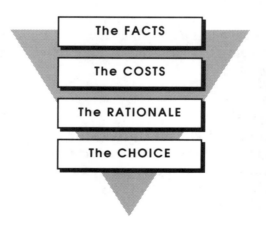

The FACTS

The COSTS

The RATIONALE

The CHOICE

Introduction

▼ A good friend of mine recently left a company and started an organization of his own. A number of clients opted to leave with him. To hear him tell the story, his departure was almost a moral responsibility. His previous employer made it a point to overcharge customers, psychologically abuse employees and boldface lie to just about anyone when it benefited the organization. Ethically he could not tolerate the situation any longer. He had to leave . . . follow his dream . . . and in some small way put the "I" back in Integrity.

Strangely enough, the employer had a distinctly different perspective. Company representatives emphatically denied the above mentioned allegations and painted a less than noteworthy professional portrait of my friend. In conversations with clients considering my friend's new organization, his former employer described his entrepreneurial activity as "illegal" and "unethical." To even consider doing business with this upstart, makeshift collection of less than professional vagabonds was condoning industrial terrorism. Starting your own company was one thing . . . but stealing clients . . . that was another!!

A series of meetings ensued. My friend queried of his former employer . . . "how does one go about _stealing_ a client?? The client is a person . . . they think . . . decipher . . . make decisions on a daily basis. If they've decided to do business with my new company . . . shouldn't we respect their collective ability to determine what's best for them?"

"Don't twist the facts," said the employer. "Those are _our_ clients. You established a relationship with them on _our_ nickel. If you want to start your own business . . . that's fine . . . but find your _own_ clients."

The ethical impasse broadened. Each side justified its position with new and creative versions of past events. Camps began to form. The stage was set. Almost simultaneously both parties opted for the age old American vehicle of conflict resolution . . . the lawsuit.

Eighteen months and eighty thousand dollars later nothing has officially been resolved. Each party has spent countless hours pouring over "boiler plate" legal jargon looking for loophole after loophole, but no official winner of the "ethics battle" has been declared.

The Facts

▼ Now I'm sure the scenario described doesn't exactly hit you as front page news . . . nor should it. In 1984, there were 13,600,000 civil lawsuits filed in state courts. That works out to a lawsuit for approximately every 17 citizens. By December of 1988, that ratio was up to a lawsuit for every 10 citizens. For the sake of comparison, Canada has a lawsuit filed for approximately every 100 citizens. In most European countries, the ratio is 1 in 1,000.[1]

As a nation, we have a better firsthand working knowledge of the legal profession than any other country in the world. We are informed about our rights on a daily basis via newspaper, radio and television advertisements. We have rights we never even knew we had . . . and we solicit legal assistance to aggressively protect them.

● For example, consider the following snapshots:

- As of June 30, 1987, there were 242,177 civil lawsuits pending in state courts. That compares to 24,453 criminal cases on file on the same date.[2]

- As of June 30, 1987, there were 13,127 civil cases pending with the United States Court of Appeals. That compares to 4,103 criminal cases being appealed as of the same date.[3]

Let's work through this for a minute. For every case commenced involving a criminal violation of justice (i.e., murder, robbery, kidnapping, etc.), there are 10 civil cases in process (i.e., patent violation, divorce, slander, etc.). For every criminal case that goes to trial and is appealed . . . there are three civil cases which go to trial and are appealed.

Now exactly what does this mean? Is it good news that for every murder there are 10 situations where my character might be defamed? Should I feel good about the fact that I'm much less likely to be assaulted with a deadly weapon than have my copyright violated? Seems like a good topic for Andy Rooney and the CBS 60 Minutes crew to look into.

One thing is for sure, if you're a lawyer, it should at least make you feel a little more comfortable about your career path. There is no reason to believe there will be any downward trend in the skyrocketing number of "cases pending" well into the foreseeable future.

Given the above, it should come as no great surprise that there are more lawyers per capita in the United States than in any other country in the world.[4] According to The American Bar Association, there were 677,584 practicing lawyers as of December, 1987.[5] Since 1950, the population of lawyers in the United States has grown twice as quickly as the population of its citizens.[6]

If you're good, becoming a lawyer is one of the most rewarding professions in the economy. Blue-chip New York law firms are paying more than $65,000 per annum to lure 25 year olds straight from the classroom. Some firms will tack on a $10,000-$20,000 bonus for working a year or two as a judge's clerk.[7] How can these firms pay these exorbitant salaries . . . EXORBITANT REVENUES.

■ Consider the following article reprinted from the September, 1986 issue of Money Magazine:

WHAT IT COSTS TO WIN A $3 LAWSUIT

Next time you consider suing your dentist for bungling a root canal or your neighbor for harboring a canine criminal that played tug-of-war with your best suit, remember that juries sometimes do the strangest things — but that lawyers almost always win. Witness the recent antitrust suit between the upstart United States Football League and the venerable National Football League. A U.S. District Court jury in New York City concluded that the NFL was a monopoly and that the USFL thus was entitled to damages. But instead of the up to $1.69 billion the USFL sought, the jury awarded its now famous $1 (trebled to $3, as is customary in antitrust judgments). But for wrangling over the $3, the three law firms hired by the NFL and the two that were employed by the USFL can expect a real windfall — at least $10 million. Some call it justice. Others might call it a legal killing.[8]

In pursuit of defining the "gray area" associated with being "right" or "wrong," it's gotten to the point where you can sue anybody for just about anything. If your lawyer is creative and convincing . . . you just might win. It's sort of like entering a judicial lottery. Whenever there's a conflict in your life or with your business . . . let the courts decide. Find yourself a purveyor of justice in a shark-skinned suit, define your position and roll the dice.

● Here is what I mean:

   – In June of 1985, there was a tenant celebrating his birthday on a Sunday afternoon who drowned when he drunkenly tried to walk along the bottom of his apartment-house swimming pool in full view of his wife and 15 friends. His wife successfully sued the landlord's insurance company.

   – In December of 1985, a man attempted suicide by jumping in front of a New York subway train. He sued the Transit Authority because the train stopped in time to save his life, but not quite soon enough to avoid some physical damage to him. He collected more than $600,000.[9]

● Tragic as the failed suicide attempt might have been, one can only imagine what a fly on the wall might have heard during the initial conversation between such a "victim" and their future legal representation:

Counsel: *So, what have you got on your mind?*

Future Plaintiff: *Well, I'm not supposed to be here and I guess that's my issue. I had a suicide planned down to the tee. I'd written letters to old girlfriends, ran all my credit cards to the limit, gotten fired from my job . . . the works. I put a lot of time, effort and energy into every detail.*

Counsel: *I can understand . . . so what happened?*

Future Plaintiff: *Well, the subway train stopped short of running me over. I got banged up pretty bad . . . but not bad enough . . . I was intending to alleviate my problems . . . not intensify them. Now I've got to pay all those credit card companies, not to mention the hospital bills I've accrued. I've suffered acute personal trauma as a result of the correspondence I'd sent anticipating my departure. I'm not going to take this lying down . . . (so to speak) . . . I demand justice!!*

Now, if you find your neck starting to bristle with disgust at the satirical tone of the last few pages, allow me the opportunity to elaborate before we continue. The intent here is not to paint a picture of the legal profession as a misguided collection of ambulance chasers making a mockery of the judicial system. By design, lawyers are in the middle of the ethical crisis. On one hand they painstakingly prosecute those that attempt to gain an unethical advantage. On the other hand, they passionately defend the same.

I would, however, suggest there is a "cause and effect" relationship between the propensity for people <u>not</u> telling the truth or trying to take unethical advantage of another party and the sheer number of civil lawsuits and lawyers in the country. By definition, the civil-justice systems' essential purpose is to resolve conflict.[10] If the number of conflicts were decreasing, it would make sense that the number of lawyers and lawsuits would also be experiencing a downward trend. As we have seen, that is anything but the case.

The ethical climate of our country is an issue . . . and one doesn't have to look very hard to find cause for concern.

■ The first two paragraphs of the May 25, 1987, cover issue of Time Magazine entitled simply "What's Wrong", pose the questions well:

> Once again it is morning in America. But this morning Wall Street financiers are nervously scanning the papers to see if their names have been linked to the insider-trading scandals. Presidential candidates are peeking through drawn curtains to make sure that reporters are not staking out their private lives. A congressional witness, deeply involved in the Reagan Administration's secret foreign policy, is huddling with his lawyers before facing inquisitors. A Washington lobbyist who once breakfasted regularly in the White House mess is brooding over his investigation by an independent counsel. In Quantico, Va., the Marines are preparing to court-martial one of their own. In Palm Springs, Calif., a husband-and-wife televangelist team, once the adored cynosures of 500,000 faithful, are beginning another day of seclusion.

Such are the scenes of morning in the scandal-scarred spring of 1987. Lamentation is in the air, and clay feet litter the ground. A relentless procession of forlorn faces assaults the nation's moral equanimity, characters linked in the public mind not by any connection between their diverse dubious deeds but by the fact that each in his or her own way has somehow seemed to betray the public trust: Oliver North, Robert McFarlane, Michael Deaver, Ivan Boesky, Gary Hart, Clayton Lonetree, Jim and Tammy Bakker, maybe Edwin Meese, perhaps even the President. Their transgressions — some grievous and some petty — run the gamut of human failings, from weakness of will to moral laxity to hypocrisy to uncontrolled avarice. But taken collectively, the heedless lack of restraint in their behavior reveals something disturbing about the national character. America, which took such back-thumping pride in its spiritual renewal, finds itself wallowing in a moral morass. Ethics often dismissed as a prissy Sunday School word, is now at the center of a new national debate. Put bluntly, has the mindless materialism of the '80s left in its wake a values vacuum?[11]

The prognosis for the future could prove to be equally unnerving. For example, in a recent survey of 131 students majoring in business, researcher John Pearce discovered that students judged the climate in American Business to be essentially unethical by a ratio of 2 to 1. Half the students accepted the idea that during their business careers, they would engage in behavior that is less than ethical.[12]

"This might not be ethical. Does that present a problem for anybody??"

The Costs

▼ Perhaps we should all take some solace in the fact that unethical behavior is still front page news. You don't hear much about the multitudes that conduct their personal and professional interactions with impeccable integrity . . . there's nothing really exciting about that, is there? And the individuals and organizations that are honest aren't really tangibly affected by those that do act unethically . . . are they??

The reality of the world is that we are all significantly impacted by the impending ethical crisis, whether we actively participate in it or sit on the sidelines with our hands over our head convincing others that there is nothing we can do.

Each year United States businesses spend nearly $20 billion on legal fees. The amount an average business spends has nearly tripled during the last decade.[13] It's to the point where you almost have to include a lawsuit or two per annum in your budget proposal. It's not so much a matter of if . . . it's a matter of when.

● Let's examine a couple of hypotheticals. Pick a situation from the following list:

- You promote somebody in your department. Another employee that did not get the promotion is suing you for discrimination.

- You want to contest a will.

- You fire an employee . . . the employee files a discrimination suit.

- You file for a divorce.

- You feel another business has violated a patent or a trademark you own.

Regardless of whether you are the Plaintiff or the Defendant, you're looking at a price tag of approximately $2700/day if your dispute goes to trial. The average cost for a court reporter to transcribe a one hour deposition is $200. Expert witnesses typically charge $300 for a written report. If you want an expert witness to testify, that will cost you $1000/day on the average.[14] Numbers like these can add up very quickly.

As a result of these costs and the increasing probabilities associated with legal involvement, one new benefit that a number of employers are offering employees is pre-paid legal services. These services offer an employee a wide range of legal work either without cost or at very low rates.

In 1978, fewer than 1.5 million people were covered by these services. Today, pre-paid legal plans cover at least 12 million. Of those, about 9 million receive the service as a benefit provided by an employer who either adopted the plan for employees or negotiated the coverage as part of a union contract. "It's a product whose time has come," says Douglas McIntosh, president of Blue Cross - Blue Shield of Rhode Island.

These plans, as you might surmise, are not cheap. Pre-paid legal agreements negotiated with the Auto Makers by the United Auto Workers cost the car companies $3 million in 1982. That cost has escalated to more than $40 million in 6 years.[15]

In addition, costs associated with liability insurance have also skyrocketed. Simply to stay in business the premiums on most policies have been adjusted to reflect the risk associated with coverage. This usually is bad bottom-line news for most businesses.

● Consider the account of Edward A. Court, president of Court Security Systems, Inc. in Van Nuys, California:

– **"In less than three years my product liability insurance has risen from $6,000/year to $40,000 per year . . . and that $40,000 buys only 10% of my 1984 coverage."**[16]

Malpractice insurance for surgeons in New York City has risen from an average of $72,000/year in 1984 to an average of $165,000/year in 1988.[17] (Food for thought the next time you fall to the floor in search of a martini after receiving a bill from your friendly local physician.)

There are other tangible costs associated with the ethical climate in corporate America, but some of the intangible or "hidden costs" appear to be much more significant. Consider the pharmaceutical industry. Pfizer Corp., with $4 billion in revenues and a strong performance in 1987, looked attractive as an undervalued stock play. But Pfizer's stock lagged the market for a reason not even hinted at in its annual reports or 10K filings — continuing legal exposure from one of its key products, Feldene, an anti-arthritis drug.

After bad publicity from England and complaints from U.S. consumer groups, the Food & Drug Administration reexamined Feldene and okayed the drug for a second time. But investors were not reassured. "There aren't any significant lawsuits now," concedes Hemant Shah, a vice president of Nomura Securities International, "but what happens if a little old lady gets Melvin Belli on her side and starts to sue?" In spite of the FDA ruling, that fear has kept Pfizer's stock trading at only 15 times earnings, compared with a multiple of 17 for the rest of the industry.[18]

The most devastating costs associated with the ethical crisis are the costs of immobility and inactivity; managers afraid to manage; teachers afraid to control their classrooms; sales representatives that avoid all risks; surgeons that won't operate.

We are all influenced by the ethical environment around us. As such, we all need to focus upon it and do all we can to reverse any disturbing trends. To quote an age old adage ". . . if you're not part of the solution . . . you're part of the problem."

The Rationale

▼ Why do people lie? Why do organizations withhold damaging information about their products from the public? Who was the first person to answer a pointed closed question with the response ". . . no comment"?

Before we jump into investigating ethical options, it probably makes sense to spend a page or two trying to pin down exactly what honesty and ethical decision making is and why some people seem to have such a tough time staying within agreed upon boundaries.

Set this book down and go ask the next ten people you see if they tell the truth. Ask them if they are honest. Ask them if they practice ethical decision making. What results would you expect? I'm guessing that 10 out of 10 will answer the above three questions in the affirmative.

Just about everyone looks in the mirror and finds a way to defend their own activity. Even if you're dealing with people that are caught red-handed . . . most folks simply do not admit a breach of ethical conduct. There are almost always a set of specific extenuating circumstances.

● Vernon Henderson, a retired minister who is an ethics consultant to the Arthur D. Little consulting firm offers a reason why:

> – **Ethical behavior is always a function of context. It is relative to a culture, an era to the pressures exerted in a given job. Standards, moreover, are in a constant flux. In a society such as ours, who's going to decide what's right and what's wrong?**[19]

Honesty - 45

As such it would appear that ethics and honesty are not a coherent set of answers, but more a coherent set of questions.

These questions arise every day. For example, manufacturers of artificial heart valves might face several difficult issues: Is it right to make a profit when someone's survival is involved? If a profit is proper, then how much profit? Is it acceptable to increase the risk of the valve's malfunctioning by a tenth of 1% to reduce manufacturing costs (and maybe, ultimately, the price) by 25%? Or is this risk simply unconscionable?

What is a reasonable level of safety when you consider a shareholder's legitimate interest in a reasonable return on investment? Even though waivers are signed before valve-implant operations, do patients whose valves fail after a certain period (or their survivors) have a legitimate grievance against the manufacturer? All too often, these are the sort of questions nobody is asking.

Business people, in particular, operate in an environment that can misshape moral consciousness. Organizational hierarchies encourage loyalty to the boss's values and objectives, rather than to one's own. Advancement often depends not on rightness of action, but on acceptable behavior and image, e.g., self-control, appearance and dress, perception as a team player and style.

The result of all this can be ethical erosion. Consider the Manville Corp., (once known as Johns Manville), a company brought down by questions of corporate ethics. More than 40 years ago, information began to reach Manville's medical department — and through it, the company's top executives — implicating asbestos inhalation as a cause of asbestosis, a debilitating lung disease, as well as lung cancer and meso-thelioma, an invariably fatal lung disease.

Manville's managers suppressed the research on their product and apparently decided to conceal the information from affected employees. This included the results of chest x-rays.

Based on such evidence, a California court found a few years ago that Manville had hidden the danger rather than look for safer ways to handle it. It was less expensive for Manville to pay workers' compensation claims than to de-velop safer working conditions. A New Jersey court was even blunter: it found that the company had made a con-scious, cold-blooded business decision to take no protective or remedial action, in flagrant violation of the rights of others.

How can we explain this behavior? Certainly not as the evil actions of a few misbegotten souls. More likely, the people involved were ordinary men and women who found themselves in a dilemma and solved it in a way that seemed the least troublesome. The consequences of what they chose to do — both to thousands of innocent people and, ulti-mately, to the corporation — probably never occurred to them.

The Manville case illustrates the difficult balance executives are expected to strike: to pursue their companies' best interests, but not overstep the bounds of what outsiders will tolerate. The problem with this situation is that even the best managers can find themselves in a bind, not knowing how far is too far.[20]

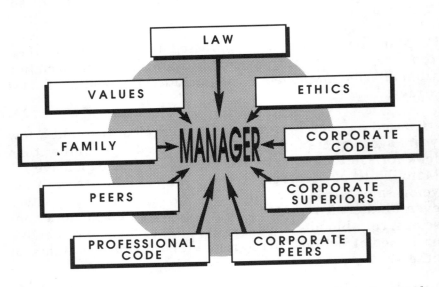

(This graphic, from the American Business Law Journal, depicts the increasing pressure on decision makers from an honesty/ethical standpoint.[21])

Individuals and organizations violate ethical decision-making practices for a variety of reasons. Fear, short-term gain, peer pressure and uncertainty are but a few. It is no longer an acceptable defense in situations of ethical misconduct that "everybody else is doing it." Coach Pete Newell makes comments on the tolerance level for cheating in college recruiting:

"When I was a little kid and I got into trouble, quite frequently I'd come home and explain to my mother '...well everybody is doing it.' I want to tell you that was the surest way to get a hit on the head. Invariably her response would be '...well you're not going to be doing it.' It's kind of amazing because that's the number one rationale I hear from college coaches rationalizing why they cheat, '...well everybody is doing it.' Well, everybody isn't doing it ...it's just a convenient rationale and quite simply ...it's not an acceptable one."

Pete Newell

If the last year or two are any indication, dishonesty and unethical decision making will receive much tighter scrutiny in the future than it has in the past. The opportunities to cheat and cut corners will still present themselves ... but the tolerance levels for unethical practices will continue to shrink.

The Choice

▼ It all boils down to choice. Your choice ... day in ... day out ... when people are looking ... and when they are not. When you find yourself in a leadership role, being honest with people is not an elective ... it's a prerequisite.

Honesty is a cornerstone in the **pyramid of influence** we will develop throughout this book ... and despite all the temptation and pressure associated with honesty ... ultimately it's something over which <u>you</u> have complete control.

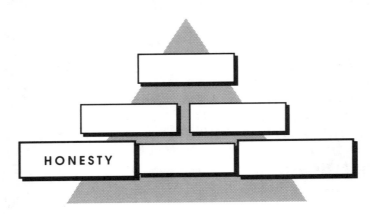

K.C. Jones offers some sage advice about the choice:

> *"It's easy to be honest with people when things are going great. The tough part about honesty is delivering the bad news ... avoiding the temptation to manage the moment and get yourself out of an uncomfortable situation. Long-term that kind of stuff will kill you."*
>
> *K.C. Jones*

Ethical checkpoints in your career inevitably will focus upon the "tough issues . . . or the tough times." It's easy to be honest when there's no pain involved. The difficulty with honesty occurs when you have a short-term opportunity to avoid pain or to reap rewards. Long-term those situations have a tendency to catch up with you.

❖ Consider a collection of quotes by and about Ivan Boesky before and after his run-in with the Securities Exchange Commission:

> *"I think greed is healthy. You can be greedy and still feel good about yourself."*
> — IVAN BOESKY, in a 1985 commencement speech at the University of California at Berkeley.

> *"If you are making a gallery of rogues, $100 million puts you pretty high up."*
> — JOHN KENNETH GALBRAITH, economist.

> *"The interesting thing about the $100 million fine is that it almost approaches the entire budget [$106 million] of the SEC."*
> — RICHARD PHILLIPS, former chairman of the American Bar Association's panel on federal securities law.

> *"Knock, knock."*
> *"Who's there?"*
> *"Ivan."*
> *"Ivan who?"*
> *"Ivan taping our conversations for the past six months."*
> — JOKE ON WALL STREET.

"You might say fear and trembling have taken the place of greed and avarice as the dominant emotions here on the Street."
— ROBERT STOVALL, president of Stovall/21st Century Advisors.

"What Boesky did [dumping his takeover stocks] is morally equivalent to selling on inside information."
— HOWARD STEIN, chairman of Dreyfus Corp.

"He's the most avaricious, arrogant piece of sewage I've ever met."
— MURIAL SLATKIN, Boesky's sister-in-law who sued him recently for allegedly misusing $14 million of funds.

"Ivan is still my friend."
— T. BOONE PICKENS JR., investor.

"What good is the moon if you can't buy it or sell it?"
— IVAN BOESKY, responding to his wife Seema's romantic comments about how beautiful Paris looked on a moonlit night, as reported in a 1984 New York Times interview.

"I happen to really believe that what I do serves the public good."
— IVAN BOESKY, in a 1985 interview.

"Honesty is the best policy."
— ANGELO ORIOLO, retired Pennsville, N.J. electrician who has filed a class-action shareholder suit over Boesky's dealings.[22]

Sooner or later you wind up paying for unethical behavior. That may mean the loss of a job, the loss of a friend or the loss of something much more important . . . your integrity. Consider the words of Claire Rothman:

"There's only one thing you have besides your persona . . . and that's your honor. Are you an honorable person to deal with? Once you lose it, you can never get it back. So you need to do everything you can to always keep it shining . . . then you never have to worry."

Claire Rothman

But what about the people that aren't honorable? What about those that I'm in competition with that don't play by the rules . . . and appear to be winning? I know that sooner or later justice will prevail . . . but what do I do in the meantime?

Usually the knee-jerk reaction to those well-intentioned questions is . . . "more structure." Thicker procedure manuals that spell out what honesty looks like and what will happen if it is not adhered to.

Before we opt for increased regulation as a strategy to insure honesty with others, let's take the opinion of Doug Collins into consideration:

"Most of the regulations that are set up in college recruiting or in business are set up for the people that have no ethics. So what happens is a committee gets together somewhere and comes up with a 2" manual that states the rules. The problem is that the people without ethics aren't going to play by the rules whether the book is 2" thick or 20" thick. You wind up punishing the people out there that are doing it the right way. That's the frustrating thing about trying to regulate dishonest people . . . all the honest people that get caught in the middle."

Doug Collins

Rules and regulations have their place when it comes to honesty and ethical decision making, and formalized codes of conduct within corporate America are certainly more evident today than they were 15 or 20 years ago.

■ W. Michael Hoffman, the founding director of The Center for Business Ethics at Bentley College recently shared his research on the establishment of "codes of ethics":

> Writing a code of ethics is an important step toward building an ethical corporation, but it's just that — a first step. To be effective, it has to be backed up by other kinds of support structures throughout the organization to ensure its adequate communication, oversight, enforcement, adjudication and review. We just didn't see this kind of support system in most of the companies we surveyed. Although 93 percent of the responding companies taking ethical steps have written codes of ethics in place — representing almost a 40 percent rise over a study for the Conference Board 20 years ago — only 18 percent have ethics committees, only 8 percent have an ethics ombudsman and only three have judiciary boards.[23]

I got a kick out of Tommy Heinsohn, CBS sports analyst and long time Boston Celtic player and coach, when he was asked about the "mystique" of the Boston Garden. His response was, ". . . as far as I know, a building has never won a game in the NBA."

It's much the same thing with formalized codes of conduct . . . the code will only be as good as the people who live by it. For example:

> In 1982, the Johnson & Johnson Company was struck with a crisis: An unknown madman laced Tylenol capsules with a deadly poison that killed seven people in Chicago.
>
> Johnson & Johnson's credo, which all managers commit to in writing, asserts that a high-quality product, commitment to the customer, equal opportunity, safe working conditions, corporate philanthropy and community responsibility are the company's highest values. Profit making is considered its final obligation. Dr. Clarence Walton, professor of ethics and the professions at The American College, says, "Anyone knowing Johnson & Johnson's corporate philosophy could have predicted the company would have risked a $120 million loss to pull Tylenol capsules from the shelves rather than risk harming customers."
>
> The crisis itself "required literally dozens of people (at Johnson & Johnson) to make hundreds of decisions in a painfully short period of time," chairman of the Board and CEO James E. Burke recalled. "Most of the decisions were complicated, involving considerable risk. And we had no historical precedent to rely on."

But throughout the ordeal, he emphasizes, "the guidance of the credo played the single most important role in our decision making. There was no way we could have instructed our people on how to make the decisions they did. Yet, somehow, they reached the same conclusions independently."[24]

Regardless of what's formally in place in your organization, honesty and ethical decision making is an individual responsibility. Sometimes lonely . . . sometimes unpopular . . . but always within grasp.

As far as advice goes, allow me to defer to those with much more experience than I:

"Through honesty you build respect . . . with respect you can build a relationship . . . with a relationship . . . you can successfully influence."

Wayne Embry

"Never do a bad act to bring about a favorable result. You don't have to cheat to win . . . it's as simple as that."

Pete Newell

"*I think about my parents almost every day and thank God they instilled in me some very basic, simple rules about dealing with people. You never lie, cheat or attempt to deceive regardless of how much you may stand to gain from it. A victory by way of deception really isn't a victory at all. Once you truly believe that, you never even think about cheating.***"**

Pat Head Summitt

"*Don't let your own comfort level dictate your morality. Just because you might feel uncomfortable letting a player go or making a tough decision, don't compound your problem by pretending it isn't there. Do what you have to do . . . get it done . . . and get on with it . . . but never compromise yourself based on what is or what isn't comfortable for you.***"**

Jerry West

If you take one thing from this book, I hope it would be a rekindled understanding of the importance of shooting straight with those you attempt to influence. Avoid the path of least resistance in "tough times." Tell people the truth, especially when it affects their future or your relationship with them. Don't sit in the stands and justify unethical behavior simply because "the system" tolerates it. Take full responsibility for acting honestly and ethically with those around you. The short-term dynamics may not always be pleasant . . . but the long-term effect will most assuredly contribute to an "improved system."

Scenario 2

(The department head that opened this chapter shares a different perspective.)

Well, I can't say I wasn't disappointed . . . that promotion would have meant a lot, no doubt about that. But, as much as I hate to admit it, I can see Joe's point. This guy from Michigan he's bringing in has the credentials and the experience to really put this place on the map.

At least Joe had the decency to put all his cards on the table and be up front about it. I could tell he was uncomfortable delivering the message. I know he wants me to do well . . . and I realize his decisions have to be made on the basis of what's best for everybody. I'll get my chance . . . and when I do, I just have to make sure I make the most of it.

▲ WORK ETHIC ▲

CHAPTER 2

▲ WORK ETHIC ▲

Scenario 1

(A 25 year employee passes on a personal perspective on upward mobility to an interested rookie.)

If you want to get to that level in the company, just realize the competition is brutal. I mean just about everybody that makes it that far is a real top management prospect. Work ethic usually separates the cream from the crop from that point on. Ability is a given . . . it boils down to how badly you want it and what you're willing to sacrifice to get it.

▲   **work eth•ic:**
         a set of principles or values regarding the exertion of effort to accomplish a task.

Overview

▼ This chapter focuses on the intangible dynamic of work ethic, effort or input. In doing so it addresses two broad categorizations of people:

- Those that don't put forth enough effort

- Those that put forth too much

The pages ahead are intended to afford you the opportunity to critically evaluate your own work ethic in light of the information presented.

Introduction

▼ The second cornerstone in our **pyramid of influence** is work ethic.

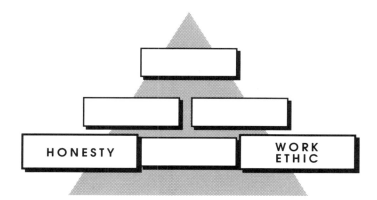

I suppose it could have been called a number of different things:

- Discipline
- Effort
- Being All You Can Be
- 110%
- Etc.

Simply stated, if you are honest . . . and consistently put in the effort and go the extra mile . . . a high probability exists that you will experience success when dealing with others.

Each of the coaches/managers we interviewed whole-heartedly concurred that success cannot be achieved without self discipline, consistent effort and day-to-day attention to detail. There is no short cut. No answer in the back of the book. No crib sheets. No easy way. Consider these comments:

"Discipline is like pregnancy . . . you either have it or you don't. You don't have a little of it . . . or have it every now and then. You've got to demonstrate it day in and day out."

Pete Newell

"I was raised in an environment where I was always expected to work hard. Sometimes I resented it. I'd go home from school and have chores to do every day while most of my friends went to the park or had a good time doing whatever. I can honestly say that the work ethic that was forced on me as a child is in large part responsible for any success I've experienced in life."

Pat Head Summitt

"For the fourteen years of my professional basketball career I ate the same meal for breakfast and for dinner before every ball game. I was almost always the first person at the arena. I took a nap at the same time every day. That to me was work ethic, or discipline. I reached an extraordinary situation within myself to make me perform every night. I knew that when I went out there on the court, if I hadn't done those things, I really felt like I had not only cheated myself, I had cheated the fans and I had cheated our team. There are similar rituals I go through as a manager . . . and I know that if I don't put in the time day in and day out to complete these rituals . . . we're not going to be successful."

Jerry West

"Applying yourself is the bottom line. I don't think anybody fails if they work hard, make the necessary sacrifices and pursue a noteworthy goal. Even if you don't succeed initially you can take that very same experience and apply it to another aspect of your life and eventually come away with a big win. The effort, or the input if you will, is the key."

Wayne Embry

"I don't think you can make a conscious effort to earn a person's respect. I think if it's a conscious effort, you're going to be acting and sooner or later get caught up in the acting and not have any idea who you really are. I think you're either sincere or you're not . . . and I know with me, the way I try to earn respect is by working hard. The players know how hard I work and how prepared we're going to be every time we walk out on the floor. Because I'm prepared and I work hard, I can expect the same from them.**"**

Doug Collins

"I know in my own career the only thing that really kept me around was excellent coaching, outstanding teammates and my willingness to work hard. I was too slow, too short and I couldn't shoot . . . I had to work harder than everybody else just to survive.**"**

K.C. Jones

"As I look back on my career, I can honestly say that I've been driven by a desire to learn as much as I possibly could about what I was doing from who-ever had the qualifications to teach me. I'm still that way. I have a need to fill my "sponge-like" head with knowledge and elicit contributions from those that know more than I. I rarely look for an easy path or accept a quick fix. Learning is work . . . it's late hours . . . meetings . . . phone calls . . . letters . . . etc. As a result of approaching my development in this manner, I was fortunate enough to bring to the table of my career accomplishments that were not coupled with 'coveting the other guy's job.' I was concentrating more on perfecting what I was doing rather than ambitiously communicating ' . . . I want to sit in your chair.' As a result, I found that I was able to sit comfortably in the number 2 or 3 chair without threatening whoever was higher up on the totem pole and eventually, got further because of it."

Claire Rothman

So, that about does it. Get out there and work hard. End of chapter . . . Right?? I'm sure we all wish it were that simple. "Work ethic," "effort," "self discipline," etc. are all terms that are easily defined on paper, but much more difficult to pinpoint in the real world. If you disagree with that assertion, run the same test suggested in the first chapter. Get out on a street corner or go down to the company lunch room and ask the first 10 people you see if they work hard . . . if they put in an honest-day's effort for an honest-day's pay. What do you think they'll tell you?

Again, 10 out of 10 would answer in the affirmative. Oh sure, occasionally you might run into an interviewee that would admit he was a doorstop . . . on cruise control . . . just going through the motions . . . but for the most part, when asked, people will tell others that they give a consistent effort day in and day out.

So what exactly is work ethic? If somebody wants to make a case that you're not working hard enough, how do they go about doing that? What are acceptable standards for evaluating work ethics? How do you measure input? What do you do when you have one follower that gets acceptable results without even trying, and another one that struggles to meet requirements but gives 110% every day of the week? Questions like these frequently elicit hazy responses.

The Input Continuum

▼   There seems to be two basic issues associated with work ethic in our society:

- The people that don't work hard enough (and would work even less if they could find a way);

- The people that work too much (and would work even more if they could find a way).

These two "work ethic mind sets" are represented below on the "Input Continuum." "Input" as a descriptor is intended to include all the terms we have utilized up to this point (work ethic; effort; discipline; etc.).

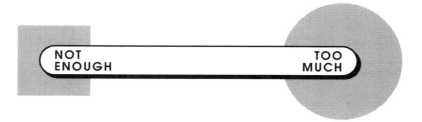

Not Enough

▼ Let's agree up front that measuring input is a qualitative nightmare with a seemingly infinite number of points of comparison.

Ever try to tell somebody that you didn't think they were working hard enough?? It can be a frustrating experience at best.

Manager: *John, I'd like to have a word with you if I could.*

John: *Sure, what's up?*

Manager: *Well, to be blunt, I just don't think you're putting as much into your job as you have in the past. Oh sure, you're here on time and you don't leave before the whistle, but . . . you seem pre-occupied . . . you're just not as focused as I know you can be.*

John: *Boy, I've got to disagree on that one. I feel like I've been working more rather than less lately. I'll admit I may not put in as much time as Jerry, but I most certainly put in a better day than Sharon . . . and she just got a merit pay increase last quarter . . . and what about Bob . . . that guy retired on active duty two years ago . . . nobody ever says anything to him.*

Because of the gray area associated with measuring input, most organizations emphasize a well documented focus on results. There's still significant room for disagreement to take place concerning "extenuating circumstances," but for the most part, the discussion is usually much more focused and much more objective.

Manager: *John, I'd like to have a word with you if I could.*

John: *Sure, what's up?*

Manager: *It's the downward trends that are starting to concern me. Based on yesterday's printout, you're projected to come in 22% below target.*

John: *Yeah, I know.*

Manager: *What's the problem?*

John: *Well, to be frank, I'm not sure . . . and I guess that's at the bottom of it. I just can't seem to put my finger on the . . .*

Lack of concentrated effort may very well be John's problem in the scenario described above . . . but it's very important to first address the observable symptoms of that problem in relation to agreed upon performance standards prior to jumping into an unsupported dissertation on John's lack of effort of late. Those kind of knee-jerk reactions can cause, rather than combat, problems.

Another issue associated with addressing a lack of input is the American Work Ethic's almost constant state of fluctuation. Simply stated, "hard work" in the 1980's doesn't compare to "hard work" 20 or 30 years ago . . . let alone during the early 1900's.

■ Consider the following description taken from David Cherrington's "The Work Ethic":

> **In the early 1900's the workweek for most occupations was at least 60 hours, and often longer. In the steel industry, for example, two men typically staffed one job around the clock. Each worked a 12-hour shift, seven days a week. The shifts rotated every two weeks, with one man having 24 hours free while the other worked 24 consecutive hours.**
>
> **In retail stores, sales personnel worked 84 hours each week — six 14-hour days. Company rules stated that the store was not to be open on Sunday except for emergencies. Salesmen were allowed one evening for courting, and two if they had attended Sunday school. Leisure hours, after a 14-hour workday, were to be spent primarily in reading worthwhile books.**[25]

Situations like these are difficult to appreciate given the individual focus of most modern day corporate benefit packages. You've got to wonder what somebody working at the turn of the century would have thought of:

- three weeks annual vacation at full salary;

- 20-25 paid holidays per annum;

- full life, medical and dental coverage;

- up to 6 months maternity leave;

- company sponsored child care centers.

Thank heaven for progress.

The other thing about the good old days is that they really weren't that long ago. The average workweek in most companies was over 50 hours until the late 1930's. A fellow by the name of Henry Ford was one of the first industrialists to reduce the work week in his factories to 40 hours and pay as much as $5 per hour in wages.[26]

His motives weren't entirely altruistic. He reasoned that by simultaneously increasing wages and leisure time there would be a significantly increased demand for automobiles. The strategy obviously worked and the standardized 40-hour work week was officially put into effect in 1938.[27]

There has also been a corresponding shift in the power relationship between "Management" and "Labor" over the years. During the 1930's and 40's, management had significantly more power than labor.

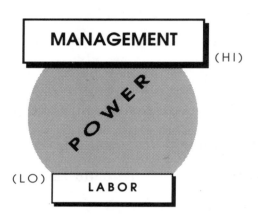

If you went to work for a company and wound up having a personality conflict with your boss, your days were numbered. "The boss" could fire you for a variety of personal or professional reasons . . . and quite frequently, "the boss" did just that.

Management, as a whole, abused their power. In response, labor organized, unionized and saw that legislation was put on the books to protect against management abusing their power in the future. A National Labor Relations Board was established forcing management to bargain in good faith. Guidelines were established and performance standards put into action.

Today, it almost seems as though the power relationship between Management and Labor has reversed itself.

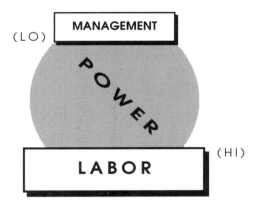

Just as Management abused the power it had during the
1930's and 40's, Labor frequently abuses the power it has in
its present day relationship.

■ Let's try to paint a contemporary picture. The following scenario took place in a manufacturing plant in the midwest:

> A supervisor was hospitalized for three weeks with a skull fracture and concussion. The incident resulted from a dispute with an employee. The supervisor claimed that the employee was intentionally working slowly to reduce the speed of the entire section. Co-workers agreed that the employee did a lot of fooling around, took extended breaks to go to the restroom or drinking fountain, and occasionally sat around doing nothing during work periods. The supervisor tried to get the employee to work faster by verbal pressure. The employee felt hassled, lost his temper, and finally struck the supervisor with a two-foot length of lead pipe. The employee was fired, the supervisor returned to work three months later, and it looked for a time as if the incident was over. Six months later, however, the company learned that it was being sued. To everyone's surprise, the company lost a lengthy legal dispute and was forced to reinstate the employee and pay back wages. As soon as he received his 22 months of back pay, he quit.[28]

Unfortunately, case studies like this actually occur on a far too frequent basis. Just about anyone tasked with the responsibility of managing others in this day and age has some kind of a "loop holes" horror story about an employee firmly implanted on the "not enough" side of the input continuum that couldn't be touched for fear of reprisal.

But it's more than a fear of retaliation that affects managers trying to cope with talented followers that give only what they "have to" to a job. It's frustrating when people don't perform up to their potential . . . when they don't put forth the effort that you know would make them successful. John Feinstein, author of the critically acclaimed book, "A Season on The Brink," was present for a dialogue between coach Bobby Knight of Indiana University and one of his players that graphically illustrates this dynamic:

> They practiced early the next morning, but without Knight: he stayed home, not wanting to put himself or his team through another emotional trauma.
>
> One morning later, Knight called Thomas into his locker room. He put his arm around Thomas and told him to sit down. He spoke softly, gently. There were no other coaches, no teammates in the room. "Daryl, I hate it when I get on you the way I did Sunday, I really do," he said. "But do you know why I do it?"

Thomas shook his head. "Because, Daryl, sometimes I think I want you to be a great player more than you want you to be a great player. And that just tears me up inside. Because there is no way you will ever be a great player unless you want it. You have the ability. But I can coach, teach, scream, and yell from now until Doomsday and you won't be any good unless you want it as bad as I do. Right now, I know you don't want it as bad as I do. Somehow, I have to convince you to feel that way. I don't know if this is the right way, but it's my way. You know it's worked for other people in the past. Try, Daryl, please try. That's all I ask. If you try just as hard as you can, I promise you it will be worth it. I know it will. Don't try for me, Daryl. Try for you."[29]

Therein lies the secret, and the beauty, of work ethic
. . . it's something over which you have 100% control. You
may not be as strong; as fast; as smart; or as slick as those
you compete against . . . but there's no reason you ever
have to take a back seat to anyone when it comes to objective evaluation of your input. Consider the comments of
Pete Newell and Pat Head Summitt:

*"I used to tell my teams on the first day of every
practice that the other team may have bigger players; they may have quicker players; they may have
smarter coaches or better shooters . . . but they will
never be better conditioned. Because that's something we always controlled . . . how hard we would
work and what kind of condition we'd be in."*
Pete Newell

*"We start out right away with a high level of ex-
pectation in our program. We expect an "A" level
performance. You simply can't get an "A" level of
performance with "C" level work standards. I don't
care how much natural talent you bring to the feast."*
Pat Head Summitt

The first chapter of this book was about the importance of being honest with others. More than anything else, this chapter is about being honest with yourself. Because only you can truly determine the extent of your input.

As was the case with Honesty, an evaluation of Work Ethic is much more a list of ongoing questions than a set of "cast in concrete" principles. For example:

- How much do you read outside normal working hours about your profession?

- How current do you stay with the developments of your industry?

- When was the last time you attended a job related seminar or clinic?

- How often do you establish specific goals aimed at improving yourself?

- Do you feel as though you've attained a stature in your profession where ". . . there's little you don't already know?"

- How many questions do you have prepared for impromptu meetings with "name people" in your field?

- How much sheer time do you put in, in comparison with your professional peers?

Of course, questions like those can only be put into context if you're clear on the role that your professional goals play in the context of your life.

As Jerry Buss, multimillionaire owner of the Los Angeles Lakers, was recently quoted as saying:

> "Anybody can become a millionaire . . . it's just a matter of what you're willing to give up in order to achieve it."

Suffice it to say that those whose "input continuums" are slanted sharply to the left will probably miss out on a number of opportunities in life.

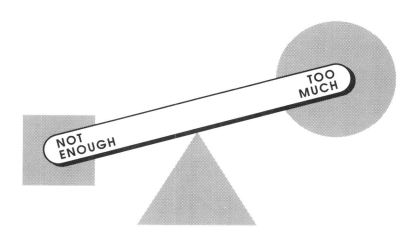

Even though those same people may wind up in situations where they can give a 50% effort and still "meet requirements," they have a tendency to cheat the organizations that employ them by not performing anywhere near their potential. Much more tragic than this, they consciously cheat themselves out of opportunities to contribute to their own self concept . . . and that, in the final analysis, is an absolute crime.

Too Much

▼ One of the great advantages of putting your thoughts down on paper is the opportunity to speak (or write, as the case may be), out of both sides of your mouth. You've just spent the last 10 minutes reading about the importance of maximizing your potential; of going the extra mile; of insuring that your personal Input Continuum doesn't skew downward and to the left.

I now ask you to critically look in the mirror and evaluate the inverse tragedy . . . the tragedy associated with putting in too much effort.

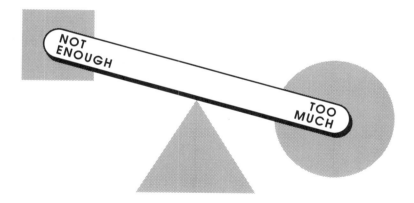

Anything to excess is an issue.

- Enjoying a good meal every now and then is one thing . . . consistently gorging yourself to the point where you are 50 pounds or more over-weight is another.

- Having an occasional beer with a couple good buddies is one thing . . . drinking until you pass out on a regular basis is another.

- Getting a tan is one thing . . . developing skin cancer as a result of over-exposure to the sun is another.

By the same token, applying yourself to your profession is one thing . . . becoming consumed by your job and ignoring all the other facets of your life is entirely different.

If you're currently in a job where you have the necessary skills to succeed, there will more than likely be a
strong correlation between the amount of effort you put
into that job and the level of productivity you attain.

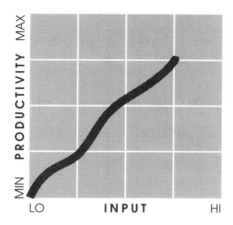

If you do your homework; stay current; ask questions;
and go the extra mile, all other things being equal, you will
experience success.

By the same token, additional input . . . past a certain point can become counter-productive.

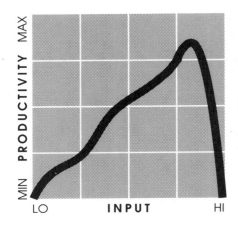

Diminishing returns set in. Productivity begins to drop off . . . or in the tragic cases where employees work themselves into "job burnout" situations, productivity can become non-existent.

"Morrison, I get the feeling you may be ready to use a couple vacation days."

Stress claims which represented only 4.7 percent of the occupational disease cases in 1980, more than doubled over the following three years and are rising steadily. It is estimated that by 1990, stress related illness could account for 20-25% of all job related illness in the United States.[30]

Those statistics fail by comparison and severity with other industrial economies around the world. In Japan, the chief executives of at least twelve major companies died from stress related illness in calendar year 1987. Most victims were in their 50's . . . the average male life expectancy in Japan is 75.

The unexpected death toll heightened the anxiety in the business community and gave the Japanese press plenty of ammunition. Story after story likened the fallen business leaders to martyred warriors. Yomiuri Shimbun, Japan's largest daily newspaper, ran a feature under these scary headlines:

SUDDEN DEATHS OF CORPORATE HEADS; DISEASE-FREE SOLDIERS UNDER HEAVY STRESS FROM RECESSION AND THE STRONG YEN.

The Sunday Mainichi referred to the trend as "death in combat."[31]

Quite possibly my "don't forget to smell the flowers" American value system is getting the best of me, but I discern a distinct difference between dying on the beaches at Normandy . . . and having a heart attack in the executive washroom.

Knocking yourself out of the game as a resource through stress related illness is but one tragedy associated with the workaholic. Consider all the missed opportunities . . . all the relationships you never had time for . . . the alimony and child support payments . . . the missed graduation parties . . . and at the end of it all, in most cases, is the loneliness.

I had the opportunity to experience what Morris Massey would refer to as a "significant emotional event" recently, while visiting my uncle, Ed Flint, in the "retirement village" he currently calls home.

Uncle Ed has long been one of the most successful people in our family. He was an accomplished athlete, coach and referee at the major college level, a retired Air Force Colonel, one of the most influential figures in the history of the Denver public school system, and an accomplished businessman besides. There is little, as far as I can see, that he has not done in life.

My visit was unannounced. I flew into Denver one day, rented a car and showed up on his doorstep. We worked our way through the surprise and shock factor of my arrival, got each other up-to-date on the latest family developments and headed for lunch.

After an extremely forgettable meal, we headed back to his apartment and were about to continue our discussion when one of his "card partners" stopped by. The man's name was Earl. He called my uncle "young fellow" because at that time my uncle was only 88. Earl never divulged his age but did mention he was born in the midst of "the gay 90's."

Earl sat down and I began to fade into the woodwork. Those two went at each other for better than an hour and a half . . . telling stories . . . taking good natured shots at each other . . . playing verbal "one ups-man-ship" . . . accusing each other of being too old to remember. It was like watching Tim Conway and Harvey Korman on a Carol Burnett Show skit.

The thing that still sticks in my mind about that visit was the content of their conversation. There sat over 175 combined years of worldly experience for ninety minutes of uninterrupted bantering, and neither of them ever mentioned a word about what they had done for a living.

They talked about shoveling snow in the midwest on cold winter mornings; their kids; their grandkids; their great-grandkids; the equipment they used to play baseball with compared with the typical battle gear donned by the present day little leaguer; etc.

As Earl struggled to his feet and made his way to the door at conversations end, I asked him what kind of business he used to be in. He looked at me with an intentionally puzzled look, chuckled and said, "You know . . . it's been so darn long . . . I can't remember."

When he was out of earshot (which unfortunately for people that age wasn't very far), my uncle told me that Earl was a retired President from a Fortune 500 firm and had served on the Board of Directors of several other organizations before calling it quits on his 75th birthday.

As much as I enjoy success; winning; competition; hard work and materialistic trappings, that day did more to put my professional work ethic into perspective than any other day I can remember. As I heard Ken Blanchard say in closing one of his seminars not too long ago, "There are very few people that lie on their death beds, look up into the eyes of their loved ones and proclaim, '. . . you know kids, if I had it to do over again, I would have worked harder and perfected the corporate re-organization plan.' "

Balance

▼ The key element in regard to work ethic is balance.

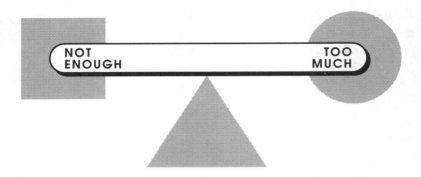

You need to find a way to put the necessary time, effort and energy into your profession, without unfavorably shifting the entire balance of your life. As was mentioned earlier, that amount of effort is something only <u>you</u> can determine.

If, after a moderate amount of "soul searching," you find yourself on the "Not Enough" side of the Input Continuum, I would suggest:

- Reading . . . block off an hour a day 5 days a week to absorb new information that's above and beyond your existing job description. Pick up professional journals; pertinent newspaper articles; files in your office you've never made time to look at, etc. Make sure this hour a day goes on your schedule and stays there. Before work . . . after work . . . at home or at the office . . . whatever makes sense given your work and home environments.

- Seminars/Discussion Groups/Conferences . . . sign up for a couple. See what the "experts" have to say. Compare their message with your reality. Force yourself into situations where you are exposed to "cutting edge" ideas or technology.

- Peer Group Discussion . . . do your best to "hang around" others in your company that know more than you do. Ask them questions . . . subtly stroke their egos . . . Listen!!

- Turning off your television . . . scrutinize your couch time. Minimize the time you spend immobilized watching others live fictional lives on a satellite dish. Watch programs and rent videos that will have a positive impact on your career.

- Challenge yourself every day when the alarm clock goes off to learn something new about your professional livelihood.

If, after the above mentioned "soul searching," you find yourself on the "Too Much" side of the Input Continuum, I would suggest:

- Getting a physical examination from a qualified medical doctor.

- Coming to grips with the importance of family and friends in the context of your life.

- Forcing yourself to take just as much vacation as your professional peers.

- Picking your kids up from school one afternoon and blowing a solid half-day running around in a park.

- Visiting an elderly relative in an old folks home.

Again, the beauty, and the tragedy associated with input is that you control it. You can make that work for you . . . or have it work against you. The choice is ultimately yours and yours alone.

Scenario 2

(A 20 year peer reminisces on the work ethic of a newly promoted
company president.)

*A lot of people like to attribute Bill's success to timing and
"breaks" at pivotal points in his career. I guess those things did
play a part. But if you ask me, the thing that has always separated Bill from the rest of us is dedication. He was tireless in his
pursuit of understanding. Always reading . . . always focused
. . . always going the extra mile. In my mind he's earned every
promotion and positioned himself for every "break" he's ever
received. This latest recognition of his efforts is no exception.*

▲ EGO ▲

CHAPTER 3

▲ EGO ▲

Scenario 1

(A less than enthused employee confides in a co-worker.)

*I can't do it . . . I just can't. I can't sit through another plan-
ning meeting and listen to Drew take all the credit for a list of
ideas he knows little or nothing about. The people in this district have been making him look like a superstar since they
painted his name on the door. You'd think once . . . just once
. . . he'd have the decency to give credit where credit is due.*

▲ e•go:
    an individual's self-esteem as compared to
    others or the world.

▲ e•go•cen•tric:
    limited in outlook or concern to one's own
    activities or needs.

Overview

▼ The role of the manager's ego is a key element in the establishment and maintenance of a productive work situation.

Ego is critical due to the ever changing nature of the work force. For the most part, followers no longer respond to managers solely on the basis of rewards and sanctions . . . there's much more involved.

As such, this chapter discusses managment ego in the context of:

- the work force

- the "coach's" role in satisfying that work force

- the development of a personalized "gameplan" to insure your ego doesn't work against you with your people.

Introduction

▼ Friday night . . . 1968. A bi-monthly El Segundo Junior High School dance just moments away. Fifty 12-14 year old disco dancing fools positioned on the steps of the El Segundo Recreation Center.

I remember this particular slice of life for two reasons. First off, I had just talked my parents into purchasing me a pair of white levi jeans. It was a tough negotiation. I went to the table and promised an "A" in Mrs. Slaughter's English class but demanded the jeans up front in time for the Friday night festivities. My father didn't like the cash in advance nature of the deal, but gave in under duress at the last minute. (Thank God for mothers.)

Following the kitchen table deliberations, I remember being poised on the steps of the Recreation Center waiting for the doors to open. Black hi-top Converse shoes . . . white jeans fresh off the rack . . . and a faded jeans jacket with the collar turned up . . . I was kind of a pre-puberty cross between Donny Osmond and Bruce Springstein . . . it was going to be a great dance . . . I could just feel it.

In the distance I saw Nita Ramsey heading my way. She was staring right at me. For a moment I thought she might be overpowered by the image I was projecting and was approaching to let me know just how fulfilled she would feel if I would spend time with her that evening.

As she drew closer . . . I could see that companionship would not be the jist of her message. This was a twelve year old on a mission.

She walked to within arms distance, squinted her eyes while simultaneously putting her right hand on her right hip, and offered the following feedback:

"Sam . . . you are just <u>so</u> conceited!!"

The spotlight was on . . . the dance now seemed a million miles away. My immediate peer group gave me their attention in anticipation of my reply. My brain was moving a mile a minute in search of a comeback that would restore my dignity. I settled on this one:

"Nita, as I see it . . . conceit is only a form of self-confidence."

Needless to say, that response didn't go over too well. I neither swayed momentum in my direction nor dampened Nita's continuing verbal barrage.

It was the only time I ever wore those "stupid" white pants and I didn't even come close to an "A" in Mrs. Slaughter's English class. All in all, it was a Friday night I really could have done without.

Be that as it may, that evening has provided a theme for this chapter . . . if you are tasked with the responsibility of influencing others . . . there is a fine line between conceit and self confidence . . . between believing in your abilities as a coach or a manager . . . and putting yourself and your opinions on a pedestal. The former is a prerequisite . . . the latter, catastrophic. In the words of Doug Collins:

"It's a player's game!!"

Doug Collins

The minute you lose sight of that assertion as a manager . . . is the minute you begin to compete with those that ultimately control your success. That can be an extremely risky strategy.

The Players

▼ People work for a variety of different reasons. Some work almost exclusively for a paycheck. Regardless of how glamorous or how repetitive the task may be . . . these folks sell their time to the highest bidder in return for wages.

Others work in order to satisfy "social" or "affiliation" needs. They like people. They like to share. They like the excitement associated with organizations. Salary will more than likely play an active role in the selection of a particular organization or job, but for the most part, these people are driven by a need to "fit in." These are the individuals that quite often turn down higher-paying jobs with other companies in order to maintain existing relationships.

Still others work because they are driven by a desire to get as much out of their jobs as they possibly can. Dollar bills may play a part in job selection . . . and they may very well enjoy those they work with . . . but the primary source of motivation for those people is the job itself.[32]

So all of us that work, whether we eat lunch from a lunch pail or sip mineral water in the executive dining room, have agendas . . . and we bring these agendas with us every day to our jobs.

```
INDIVIDUAL
AGENDAS
   • Fame
   • Fortune
   • Affiliation
```

Organizations also have agendas. Profit margins . . . stockholder satisfaction . . . return on investment . . . new product development and corporate image to name a few. There are a series of "end results" that organizations must accomplish on an ongoing basis in order to remain in business.

ORGANIZATIONAL AGENDAS

- Profit
- ROI
- New Product Dev.

The integration of individual and organizational agendas usually dictates employee tenure and organizational viability. Simply stated, if the organization can't recruit and keep good people . . . it's chances for survival are slim . . . and if employees can't find a way to satisfy their individual needs . . . it's a good bet they won't stick around too long. A graphic representation of that kind of a relationship might look something like this:

INDIVIDUAL AGENDAS

ORGANIZATIONAL AGENDAS

However, if organizations can find a way to satisfy the needs of it's individuals,

there is a strong possibility that both entities will benefit from the relationship. All other things being equal, the organization is positioned to prosper and the individual is satisfied making an active contribution to that prosperity.

Happy people are productive people!! No earth shattering news there. But worker satisfaction can be a complex dynamic. What does it look like exactly? How do you go about achieving it if it's not already alive and well? Look, we have a job to do . . . how much time can we afford to spend running around trying to figure out how "satisfied" everybody is?

● One of the foremost authorities on worker satisfaction in the behavioral sciences is Frederick Herzberg from the University of Utah. His research has been conducted world wide in a myriad of different public and private organizations over a period of thirty years.

In what Herzberg made famous as his "Motivation/ Hygiene Theory," he found that the things that "turned employees on" about their jobs were quite different than the things that "turned employees off." Stated another way, the opposite of "job satisfaction" is not "job dissatisfaction" . . . but "no job satisfaction."[33]

Based on his studies, Herzberg concluded that approximately 80% of the factors in <u>satisfying</u> job events come from the intrinsic elements of the job. These factors are things like:

- A sense of achievement

- Recognition for achievement

- The work itself

- Responsibility

- Advancement

- Personal Growth

Herzberg also concluded that approximately 70% of the factors in <u>dissatisfying</u> job events come from the extrinsic elements of the job. These factors are things like:

- Company policy and administration

- Supervision

- Relationships with co-workers

- Working conditions

- Salary

- Job Security

In an attempt to validate these assertions, run this simple test the next time you have a chance. Ask the people that report to you to take out a sheet of paper and write down their answers to the following question:

> **"What was the most <u>satisfying</u> experience in the last two years of your professional career . . . and why?"**

When they've finished, ask them to take out another sheet of paper and answer the following question:

> **"What was the most dissatisfying experience in the last two years of your professional career . . . and why?"**

In most cases the answers to the first question will be things like:

- Making 110% of my goal in the midst of significant downward industry trends.

- Being named employee of the year.

- My promotion to department head.

True satisfaction seems to be internally driven. Things that "I" did or that "we" accomplished as a team.

By contrast, most of the answers to the second question will be things like:

- A re-organization of the company that forced me to move my family to keep my job.

- Working for the worst supervisor I've ever had in my life.

- Working in hazardous conditions due to out-dated equipment.

- Living in constant fear of a hostile takeover accompanied by a reduction in forces.

True dissatisfaction is usually driven by things that are out of our control. Things that "they" did. "They" might refer to a group of faceless board members thousands of miles away, or a group of co-workers that just ramrodded a policy change through channels that will adversely affect your job.

The Coach's Role

▼ So, . . . you're a "manager" and you have 8 to 12 "workers" that "report to you." Some are driven by security needs . . . some by a need for affiliation . . . some by "striving to be all they can be." Some might be fresh off their "most satisfying professional experience" . . . while others have just worked their way through their "most dissatisfying experience."

So what? I mean . . . what, if anything, does all that have to do with you? Why should <u>you</u> care what drives the people that work for you? As long as you're meeting quota this month, why should <u>you</u> care about where <u>your</u> people are coming from?

Questions like these really get at the heart of the changing role of the manager in this day and age. The next few pages will address that transition in the context of:

- Short-term Success vs. Long-Term Effectiveness

- Power

- Knowledge

- Upward Mobility

● Short-Term Success vs. Long-Term Effectiveness ●

The "coach" is ultimately responsible for the level of worker satisfaction. However, the "coach" is also responsible for producing acceptable end results. Achieving one at the expense of the other is most often unacceptable.

Let's take a look at the way most coaches attack these responsibilities. Typically, they initiate action with their followers by attempting to influence them in a direction consistent with the goals or agendas of the organization.

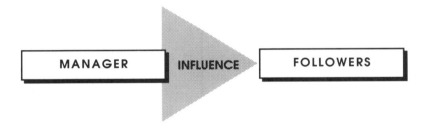

MANAGER INFLUENCE FOLLOWERS

As a result of this influence attempt, the manager is either successful or unsuccessful. The job either gets done to perfection . . . nowhere near perfection . . . or somewhere in between.[34]

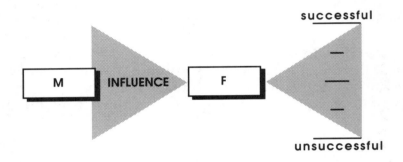

Right, wrong or indifferent . . . coaches and managers are usually evaluated much more critically on their ability to produce end results, than on any other aspect of their job.

Rarely does the coach of the undefeated National Championship team get fired because the players on that team had low levels of overall worker satisfaction. Rarely does the sales manager in the Fortune 500 firm get axed when his/her region comes in at 118% of target. Organizations simply cannot survive without successful end results and they tend to reward the managers that can produce them.

On the other hand, managers that drive their people into the ground in order to attain positive end results defeat their own purpose. It doesn't do the coach of the undefeated National Championship team much good if his/her players transfer to other schools and refuse to assist in the recruiting effort of the incoming class. It's little consolation to the sales manager at 118% of target when all the sales representatives in the region quit and hire on with competitive firms.

For these reasons it's important to give managers a report card not only on short-term success, but also on long-term effectiveness.

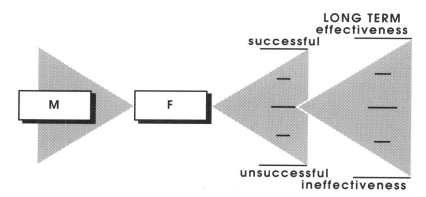

The effectiveness dimension relates to the level of worker satisfaction present in the system. It's important not only for the team to win the National Title . . . but to feel good about the sacrifices they've had to make to get there. It's important not only for sales representatives to come in over target at the end of the quarter . . . but to feel good about that contribution, and excited about the opportunity to do even better over the next 90 days.

The manager has a crucial role in both short-term success and in long-term effectiveness. It is a crucial role because each manager bears individual responsibility for creating an environment that encourages his/her followers to achieve desired end results, and feel good about the process of doing so. It's a crucial role because it's a role that is in an almost constant state of transition.

It's tougher to manage others today than it was 10 years ago. It's tougher because managers have less power . . . and followers have more. It's tougher because in many cases manager's have less technical expertise . . . and followers have more. It's tougher because there are fewer and fewer reliable blueprints on how to "get ahead."

● Power ●

During our interview, Jerry West had a tendency to reflect quite a bit on his playing career. One such reflection stood out for me as I sat down to put this chapter together:

> **"**I constantly hear about one player or another having publicized "difficulty" with their coach. You know, 'I don't like this' or 'I don't like that' . . . etc. That kind of thing was just so foreign to me as a player. There was no one I ever played for that I didn't like and respect as a coach. I thought it was a selfish attitude not to try to understand that each coach has a different way. Each coach had a different appeal . . . and it was up to me to take my ego and put it in the background and do whatever that coach wanted me to do. As a player, I took great pride in that ability.**"**
>
> *Jerry West*

More than anything else, the thing that caught my attention about Jerry's comment was how much it differed from what you typically hear about today's superstar athlete:

- Superstar Contract Re-negotiation on the Horizon!!

- Superstar vows arbitration if demands not met!!

- "Play me or trade me," says disgruntled superstar!!

It makes you long for the good old days. Players like West, K.C. Jones, Wayne Embry, Doug Collins, Bart Starr, Sandy Koulfax, Roberto Clemente and Johnny Unitas playing their hearts out win, lose or draw.

Along with those players, coaches like Vince Lombardi, Red Auerbach and Earl Weaver ranting and raving on the sidelines or in the dugout . . . calling all the shots . . . pushing all the right buttons . . . and throwing cigars to appreciative crowds when victory was in hand. Now <u>those</u> were superstars!!   And <u>those</u> were superstar managers!!

Who will ever forget Vince Lombardi's well documented negotiation with the first player agent to ever approach his office on behalf of a Green Bay Packer.

The Packers had won the 1967 Super Bowl. In his final words to the World Champions, Lombardi published his views on off season negotiations with "player agents":

Lombardi: *I've heard rumors that a few of you have signed contracts with agents . . . and that these agents will be approaching the Packer organization on your behalf to renegotiate your contracts. I want to be perfectly clear on the subject . . . the Packers will not renegotiate any contract currently in effect and I will not discuss anything whatsoever with an agent!!*

Most of the Packers knew Lombardi to be a man of his word. But there wouldn't be a story here if at least one hadn't doubted it.

That Packer was an all-pro center by the name of Jim Ringo. Mr. Ringo had two seasons left on his existing contract. He agreed to terms with an agent and sent said agent in to re-negotiate his contract with the General Manager/Coach of the Packers . . . Mr. Lombardi.

The agent showed up at Coach Lombardi's office one morning and identified himself to the receptionist. The receptionist buzzed Coach Lombardi and said, "Mr. Nelson, a player agent for Jim Ringo is here and would like to speak with you." "Tell him to sit down and wait for a minute," a gruffled Lombardi barked.

Mr. Nelson took a seat by the receptionist's desk and patiently paged through a Packer's publication. About ten minutes later a smiling Lombardi came out of his office and extended his hand.

Lombardi: *Good morning, Mr. Nelson. Thanks very much for stopping by, but I'm afraid you're visiting the wrong team. Jim Ringo has just been traded to the Philadelphia Eagles!*

Unfortunately, (or fortunately if you happen to be a player agent in Green Bay, Wisconsin), the days of the management power play are all but gone. Coaches are almost like interchangeable parts. Here today . . . gone tomorrow. Player agents and arbitration are as big a part of the modern day athletic industry as stat sheets and equipment managers.

The world of work has survived similar transitions. As was detailed in the preceding chapter, managers used to wield Lombardi like power in organizations. Their word was law . . . and you had better obey it.

Mutual <u>M</u>anagement <u>B</u>y <u>O</u>bjectives performance discussions have replaced traditionally dictatorial boss to subordinate performance review sessions. Followers, in many cases, tell managers what they plan to accomplish and highlight specific areas where the managers might be able to assist them in achieving their targets.

In addition, many organizations have done away with formal review sessions altogether. No executive washrooms or parking spaces . . . no special dining rooms . . . everyone calls everyone else "associate" . . . tenure is less and less a consideration . . . and the power of creative applicability has all but replaced the power of tenured legitimacy.

● Knowledge ●

It's tougher to keep up to speed on things these days too. Oh sure, technically sophisticated computers allow you to store more information, retrieve it quicker and process it better. Phone systems have conference calling, call waiting, call forwarding and a variety of other features. Sophisticated message systems facilitate 24-hour accessibility, along with a host of many other systems and gadgets geared to insure the efficiency of the contemporary manager.

The fact of the matter is that managers have access to so much data, they frequently can't decipher the important information from the information that has little or no impact. The catch all descriptor for such predicaments is "information overload."

Information overload simply was not as big an issue 10-15 years ago. "The boss" had access to relevant facts and made decisions. A typical organizational structure might look something like this:

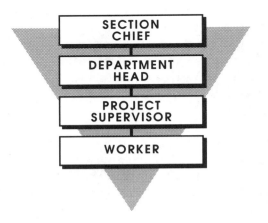

The further up the ladder you progressed . . . the more information/knowledge you accumulated . . . the more decisions you had the opportunity to make.

If a situation arose that was not covered by the company policy and procedure manual, you alerted your boss. If your boss didn't have an answer, he alerted his boss . . . and so on.

Most successful contemporary organizations cannot operate in such a procedurally emphasized manner. They do have policies and procedures . . . but they emphasize flexibility. They feature decentralized, on-line decision making employees. They put a premium on the quality and quickness of their responses to unforeseen issues. Structurally, such an organization might look something like this.[35]

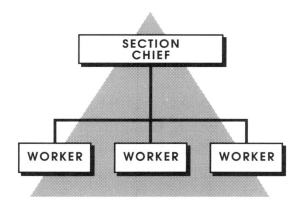

In order to survive in such a system, the manager virtually <u>has</u> to trust his/her followers' decision making capability. Followers in such a system may very well wind up possessing more content knowledge and/or technical expertise than their supervisors. The boss is no longer always the expert, the resource and the decision maker. The boss is part of the system set up to service customers and pursue competitive advantage.

● Upward Mobility ●

Getting ahead in the organization has also taken on a distinctly different meaning. Historically, becoming upwardly mobile was fairly basic. You pleased your boss and you made sure your direct reports did the same for you.

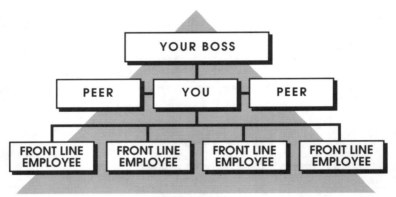

The focus was <u>up</u> in the organization . . . how can I utilize the resources available to me to impress my boss in comparison with my professional peers so that I can move to the next level on the pyramid? As a result, you had people in organizations running around doing everything they could do to respond to their boss' specific needs.

The Tom Peters induced "Excellence Revolution" has re-defined the focus in most contemporary organizations. Impressing your boss is still the objective . . . but the method is decidedly different.

The mentality of the excellence movement goes something like this:

- Customers are important. They are the reason we are in business in the first place. We will do everything within our power to insure that our customers are highly satisfied with our products and our services.

- Typically customers come in contact with first level employees. As such, we need to do every thing we can to insure these first level employees are competent and committed to our organization. In so doing, we're betting on the fact that satisfied first level employees will insure long-term customer satisfaction.

When these statements of purpose become operational-ized, a funny thing happens to the traditional organiza-tional structure. The focus is now on what you can do for your followers and your customers . . . as opposed to what you can do for your boss.

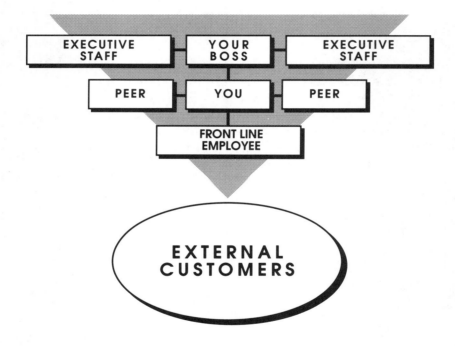

The resultant effects of an organization behaving in accordance with such a mentality are usually three fold:[36]

- Content customers

- Successful and effective followers

- Happy bosses

Managing in such an environment is unquestionably a challenge. The John Wayne, Vince Lombardi and General George Patton role models have served their purposes and have faded into the sunset. They have been replaced by the customer hugging, employee cheerleading antics of people like Mary Kay Ash (Mary Kay Cosmetics) and Stew Leonard (Leonard Grocers).[37]

The managers/coaches we interviewed had intuitively grasped that reality long ago. Consider their comments on the present day role of the coach in relation to "Players," "Success," "Power," "Knowledge," and "Upward Mobility":

"I have a lot of confidence in my ability to coach this game. I have an ego too . . . but that ego usually stays pretty quiet. I guess I liken it to the relationship between a jockey and a horse. In any given day a jockey might ride 5-6 different horses. Now, who adjusts to who? Does the horse adjust to the jockey or does the jockey adjust to the horse? From my perspective it's always the jockey that adjusts to the horse. That's the one who's got the talent. That's the one that's out there doing the running. The minute you lose sight of that is the minute you get yourself into serious trouble."

K.C. Jones

"Whenever I start thinking that I'm in the center of the circle and I'm kind of overstating my role or my contribution to our success, I try to think about a quote I heard from the author, Alex Haley. He said, 'If you ever see a turtle sitting on a fence post, you know he didn't get there by himself'."

Pat Head Summitt

"The one thing I've come to know very well in the relatively short period of time I've been a coach is that the players don't want to win nearly as bad as I do. It's not that they don't care, or that losing doesn't hurt them . . . it's just that it fails by comparison. You know, I'm the coach, my signature is on this team . . . so when we lose . . . it's a big deal to me. As long as I keep that in perspective it helps me to keep my ego from going out of control and alienating the people that in the final analysis are my livelihood."

Doug Collins

"As a manager you've got to accept the fact that you're not going to get any credit. The players, the owner . . . they get the credit. You can't let yourself get into competition for that credit . . . there simply isn't enough of it to go around."

Jerry West

"As a manger I do everything I can do to keep myself out of a competitive relationship with the players. It's their game. They have to get the job done and I have to relinquish my ego. It's as simple as that."

Wayne Embry

"If the players on our team don't want to work hard for me . . . ultimately they can get me fired. I know that and they know that. As long as I keep that in the front of my mind when I get ticked off at one of them . . . I'm ok."

Doug Collins

Ego - 125

● Managers like these somehow seem to find a way to successfully walk the tightrope between self-confidence . . . and self destruction. They seem to never lose sight of the fact that these players ultimately will dictate their success. As such, they do everything they can possibly do to create an environment that encourages their players to excel. They remove sources of dissatisfaction. They take a back seat when it comes to praise and recognition. Instead of "walking tall and carrying a big stick," they find a way to give credit where credit is due and fade into the wood-work when the spotlight is on.

"Rumor has it the authority of his new position has gone to his head."

The Game Plan

▼ If your workers aren't as satisfied as they could be . . .
if your ego has a tendency to get in the way of your own
eventual success . . . if you have difficulty keeping good
people around . . . there are some things you can do to
better position yourself and increase your future probabilities for success. In order of importance, those things
are:

- Get Your Own Act Together

- Hire Good People

- Get Out Of Their Way

● Get Your Own Act Together ●

Not too long ago I happened to be present when Ken Blanchard was informally expounding on the reason so many poor managers still exist in our economy. His discussion went something like this:

Blanchard: "Quite often the underlying cause responsible for poor management technique is insecurity. If I don't have my own act together . . . if I'm not feeling ok about myself . . . it's pretty difficult for me to feel ok about the people working for me. In fact, I'm likely to view those working for me as a threat, because if they don't perform, they can validate my feelings of inadequacy."

Most of us experience periodic fluctuation with our individual "coefficients of self confidence." A certain amount of internal questioning is normal. I like Claire Rothman's analysis of this dynamic:

"Periodically I suffer from what I call the "imposter complex" . . . you know, do I really know what I'm doing or am I just a good con-woman?"
Claire Rothman

Fluctuating self confidence is one thing . . . legitimate self doubt is another. It's safe to say that if you sincerely lack confidence in your ability to lead, manage, parent, negotiate . . . any situation where other people are involved, it's only a matter of time before that insecurity is passed along to others . . . and the only thing worse than not having confidence in yourself is to realize that the people working for you don't have any confidence in you either.

Two tidbits of sage advice on this matter. One pro-active and one reactive:

>Pro-active: Do all you can to develop skills in the "technical," "administrative" and "people" arenas of your job.

>TECHNICAL — Read, explore, ask questions, review your industry's history . . . become a student of your profession.

>ADMINISTRATIVE — Get up to speed on your organization's policies and procedures. Brainstorm ways these time-tested rules and regulations can work for you or assist you in your efforts to create a positive work environment.

<u>PEOPLE</u> — Go to seminars. Think through potentially "touchy" situations before you act. Be spontaneous with rewards and calculating with reprisals. Diagnose your situation <u>before</u> you act. Don't rely on your comfort zone or what has worked in the past.

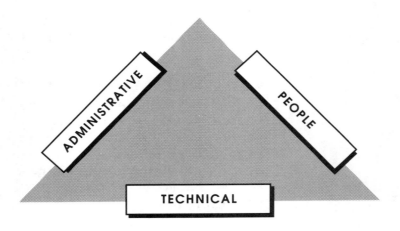

By learning as much as you can about these three separate but interactive elements of your responsibilities, you
can pro-actively combat future battles with the "imposter
complex."

Reactive: When you do find yourself in situations
that you don't know much about . . .
and you're feeling insecure . . . admit
it!! Confide in a peer. Seek assistance
from your boss. Level with your followers. Confront your insecurity and
try to work through it. Don't try to
dance around it or pretend it doesn't
exist. Odds are you won't fool too many
people anyway. You'll wind up com-
pounding your problem by creating a
whole new set of integrity issues that
need to be dealt with.

● Hire Good People ●

Spend more rather than less time on the interviewing/ hiring process. Make sure you're in sync with those you bring on board. Don't succumb to the pressure to get a "warm body" into a vacant spot.

I came across the following quote from George Allen, former head coach of the Washington Redskins, that seemed to address this issue:

> "Look beyond the resume in making hiring decisions. Look for more than ability. If a player or an assistant coach came in talking about money or retirement benefits . . . I wrote him off. I wanted to hear how he was going to help us win."[38]

Claire Rothman had a couple thoughts that reinforce the importance of hiring the best:

"Surround yourself with the best possible person to do each job. Never be afraid of expertise. If you're good . . . you'll motivate them to bigger and better things. If there's no room for them to grow bigger and better in your organization, they'll move on and bring you back laurels. Always aim for the best possible person for each area of responsibility and you'll have the strongest and best team.

If you find yourself afraid of expertise around you, then I think it's a sign that you really don't belong where you are. You've got to have confidence in your ability to select and keep good people. Managers that surround themselves with mediocre people insure mediocre results."

Claire Rothman

● Get Out Of Their Way ●

If you've got confidence in yourself as a manager, and you've put together a team of the best possible resources, the final hurdle is to step back and let your followers drive the process. This doesn't mean you never intervene . . . or instruct . . . or counsel . . . it simply means you need to ease up the reins and let your thoroughbreds get moving around the track.

Harvey MacKay gets at this dynamic in his best selling book, "Swim With the Sharks . . . Without Being Eaten Alive." He states there are four things you need to do to build a successful business.

1) Find the capital

2) Find a favorable environment to employ it

3) Hire key people

4) Know when to get the hell out of the way[39]

Establishing and maintaining a positive work environment is essential for productivity and long-term commitment. Next to being honest with others, and applying yourself day in and day out, relinquishing your ego is a crucial element that can dictate your success and effectiveness. It is also a dynamic over which you have ultimate control.

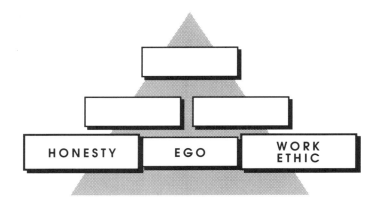

Scenario 2

(A promotion party spokesperson passes along best wishes to a
newly promoted Vice President.)

*". . . and you know, Jenny, all kidding aside, you gave us the
opportunity to really believe in ourselves and in this company.
You consistently took full responsibility for our failures and
conscientiously gave each and every one of us full credit for our
success. You made us a team . . . and everyone had the opportunity at one time or another to be team captain. We thank you
for that, and we wish you nothing but continued success. Sincere congratulations on your promotion . . . and may there be
many more to come."*

▲ WINNING & LOSING ▲

CHAPTER 4

▲ W I N N I N G & L O S I N G ▲

Scenario 1

(An opinion is offered from one long time professional acquaintance
to another.)

*A.J. and I came into this company together. He was a good
friend . . . helped me out on more than one occasion. He was bright
. . . knew what to say, when to say it . . . all that stuff.*

*Top management saw his talent too. He moved through the
ranks like he had a jet pack strapped to his back. Seems like every
time we sat down at a meeting he had a new title.*

*But something happened to A.J. during that climb. He lost
touch. Started becoming part of the problem he set out trying to
solve. Wound up stepping on a lot of toes, making a lot of enemies
and getting into a lot of win-lose power struggles.*

*I certainly wasn't surprised to hear that he'd been let go . . . in
a way . . . it was inevitable.*

▲ **win•ning:**
 **achieving success; accomplishing sought af-
 ter goals.**

▲ **los•ing:**
 failing; coming up short of sought after goals.

Overview

▼ Whether it's putting a team on the floor to challenge for an N.B.A. title or putting a proposal in a customer's "in" basket to challenge for an upcoming bid, winning and losing are the inevitable results of engaging in any kind of competition.

This chapter attempts to differentiate between true winners and losers . . . between success and failure. It investigates the short- and long-term ramifications of competition and offers advice on how to establish healthy perspectives in competition.

Introduction

▼ <u>WINNING</u>!! . . . <u>SUCCESS</u>!! . . . the mere mention of the words brings images to mind:

- The United States Hockey Team hugging each other on the ice after their stunning victory over the Soviets in the 1976 Olympics.

- Jesse Jackson addressing the 1988 Democratic National Convention and declaring a long sought after victory for civil rights in this country.

- Bobby Knight on the shoulders of his team leaving the court after a convincing gold medal thrashing of Spain in the 1984 Summer Games.

- Michael Jackson with an audience full of "beautiful people" in his hip pocket as he debuts his "Man in the Mirror" single at the 1988 Grammy awards.

Our society is keenly focused on achieving success. In many walks of life, success isn't a goal . . . it's a given. We strive for it . . . pay big bucks to position ourselves to attain it . . . sneer at those who can't handle it . . . quickly disregard those who outlive it . . . and eulogize those who describe the pursuit of it. Remember this one?

"Winning isn't everything . . . it's the only thing."

(Paul Bear Bryant, Head Coach Alabama Crimson Tide, 1958 - 1982)

In similar fashion, the terms <u>losing</u> . . . or <u>failure</u> bring distinctly different images to mind:

- Jim and Tammy Baker avoiding reporters outside their Palm Springs estate.

- Richard Nixon's resignation speech in 1972.

- A tearful Jimmy Swaggert confessing his sins to his congregation.

- An eerie looking Charles Manson peering through the bars of his cell into a camera for yet another in a series of television programs documenting his perversion.

- Roberto Duran in the twilight of a brilliant boxing career exhaustingly holding up his right hand and proclaiming . . . No mas . . . No mas.

Our society has little tolerance for losers. It's a fate to be avoided at all costs. Losers are scorned . . . pitied . . . chewed up . . . spit out . . . and worst of all . . . forgotten. Losing frustrates some, and intimidates others. It is a sober and inescapable destiny for those willing to compete. For every high side . . . there is a down side. For every hill . . . a valley. For every champagne cork popped in a victorious locker room there is a towel thrown to the floor in disgust by a member of the team that came up a little short. For every famous quote aimed at describing the importance of victory, an equally famous phrase detests the impact of defeat.

"Show me a good loser . . . and I'll show you a loser!"

(Woody Hayes, Head Coach Ohio State Buckeyes, 1951 - 1978)

■ Jim Valvano, basketball coach of the North Carolina State Wolfpack, tells a story in many of his speaking engagements that captures the essence of the difference between winning and losing:

> There is a famous football coach from our part of the country that won a national championship a few years back. His team went 12-0. Undefeated, untied and untouched. Won a big bowl game on New Year's Day. Had the kind of season a coach dreams about.
>
> Well, there was an alumni dinner in honor of that coach and his team in their home state a couple days after the final rankings became official. The place was packed . . . people were still patting each other on the back congratulating themselves on the greatest season ever in the school's history.
>
> After a banquet fit for a king, the coach was summoned to address the crowd. His name was announced and the whole place went crazy . . . gave him an extended standing ovation . . . played the school fight song . . . the works.

When the hoopla died down a little bit, the coach picked up the microphone and greeted the crowd by saying:

'I sure appreciate all this . . . but what happens if we go 4-8 next year?'

A supportive voice from the crowd immediately answered:

'We'll still love you, coach.'

A more pragmatic supporter then chimed in:

'Ya . . . and we'll miss you too.'

Perspective

▼ Winners were interviewed for this book. Proven winners. Whether they coached at the college level, professional level, were general managers or a President of a major sports facility. . . all of them had distinguished themselves in comparison with their professional peers.

Frankly, the notion of exploring the subject of failure with this crew seemed a little far-fetched. I anticipated a gruff remark or two, then a subtle but quick transition into a more comfortable topic area. As it turned out, that was anything but the case.

The interviewees almost jumped at the opportunity to discuss their past shortcomings . . . the taunts of angry fans . . . the seasons where the alumni almost ran them out of town . . . the press that cryptically evaluated their every move . . . and in the end, the players and the fans that stuck by them through thick and thin.

The word that came up at least once in every interview was "perspective." Things all had to be put into "perspective" . . . and "perspective" was something that each of them defined for themselves. No fans, no press, no participative process . . . they each determined the parameters for what they would consider victory . . . or what they would admit was defeat.

It is in this context that "Winning and Losing" was chosen as a major topic area for this book.

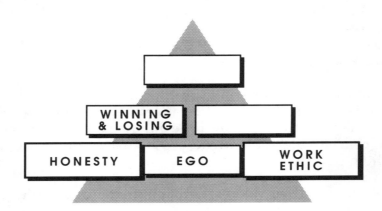

As a manager, a parent, a sales representative or union chief, the minute you get too wrapped up in your victories, or too depressed after your losses, is the minute you begin to lose touch with reality. As we all know, that can be an extremely difficult tightrope on which to maintain your balance.

As was detailed in the INTRODUCTION chapter, Pete Newell had an N.I.T. championship team, an NCAA championship team and coached what many experts describe as "the best Olympic Basketball team in history" in 1960. With all that on his resume, Pete Newell talked more about his 1954-55 University of California team than any other squad he ever put on the floor. (By the way, that team had a 1-11 record.)

Consider the reflections of Coach Newell:

"The thing about that team I'll never forget was the fact that we never despaired. We were young . . . one senior and four sophomores in our starting five. We lost games every way you could figure as young teams will do . . . it seems like young teams invent ways to lose games. But through it all we kind of hung our hat on the fact that we were young and you'd better take your shots at us now. Well, the following season we turned our won-loss record around . . . and the season after that these same players wound up winning the championship. Then we went on to win it four years in a row . . . but I credit any success we had at Cal with that 1-11 team in 54-55 . . . because they gave us the fiber to go on and create a very successful basketball period at Berkeley."

Pete Newell

Claire Rothman takes the failure-success analogy a step further:

"I think one should prepare themselves for failure. Failure is the doorstep to success. You have to fail, otherwise you're never going to learn anything. I've had some dreadful failures in my life, some horrible insecurities, some grim and black fears. But every time I hit the lowest point, I've risen the highest. I look at my life as a series of plateaus. Sometimes it levels off for a little while, sometimes I run into a little rut here and there, but overall it evens out.

Failure is really nothing to be afraid of as long as it's an honorable failure, as long as you didn't cheat, as long as you didn't steal, as long as you didn't destroy somebody. You have a right to fail. You have as much right to fail as you do to succeed. One is only the flip side of the other. You should not be afraid. Fear is a natural thing because everybody wants to succeed at everything they do. Not only do we want to succeed, but we want to do it better than anybody else could do it. Do others fall flat sometimes? Absolutely. The main thing is what can you learn from it? Where did it go wrong? Did you not put enough effort in? Did you not have enough information? Are you wise enough to know the difference between what you can control and what you can't?"

Claire Rothman

Jerry West is short and to the point when the subject of failure and management comes up:

"I think fear of failure motivates people to do extraordinary things. By the same token, not being able to handle failure once it's occurred is a real deterrent to any future opportunities you may have. I think if you are the type of person that gets intimidated by failure, you probably don't belong in a leadership capacity."

Jerry West

Pat Head Summitt offers tactical advice:

"We have a rule at Tennessee . . . you get 24 hours before a game to think about that game . . . you get 24 hours after that game to reflect on it's outcome . . . win, lose or draw. It's not a perfect system, but it tends to keep us realistic after the wins and optimistic after the losses."

Pat Head Summitt

Each of the managers interviewed seemed to garner a special strength from defeat. It toughened them . . . it forced them to develop resiliency. It taught them to truly appreciate the success to which they would become accustomed. In the final analysis, it's one of the key characteristics that separates them from others.

Much has been written over the years about winners and losers. A host of different definitions are floating around for each. The best I've run into were developed by Muriel James and Dorothy Jongeward in their time tested classic "Born to Win."

> **"Winners are those who respond authentically by being credible, trustworthy, responsive and genuine. Losers are those that fail to respond authentically."**[40]

Authentic people look inward to develop perspective. They realize that winning is not so much a function of final outcome, as it is a function of how closely performance matches up to potential.

Winners live in the present, with an eye on the future while learning from their past. Winners know their limitations . . . they can separate their strengths from their weaknesses, and they have the ability to respect both.

On the other hand, true losers seldom live in the present. They bemoan their past and are intimidated by their future. They play games with themselves and with anybody else who will join them. You may have heard some of these lines from losers explaining their misfortune:

If only I had married someone else . . .

If only I had a different job . . .

If only I had finished school . . .

If only I had been handsome (beautiful) . . .

If only I had been born rich . . .

If only I had had better parents . . .

Or these from losers procrastinating opportunities away while they wait . . . and wait . . . and wait:

When school is over . . .

When Prince Charming or the ideal woman finally comes . . .

When the kids grow up . . .

When that new job opens . . .

When the boss dies . . .

When my ship comes in . . .

Or these from losers who have gloomy crystal balls:

What if I lose my job . . .

What if I lose my mind . . .

What if something falls on me . . .

What if I break my leg . . .

What if they don't like me . . .

What if I make a mistake . . .[41]

Losers simply never give themselves the opportunity to win.

Getting the most out of your natural talents . . . that's what winning is all about. Take your God given gifts and position yourself to make a difference. Individual outcomes are almost inconsequential . . . taking full advantage of what you bring to the feast is the name of the game.

● I learned a vivid lesson from a true winner about 12 years ago. It took place on the steps of Michel Hall (the campus hospital) at the United States Coast Guard Academy in New London, Connecticut. I had just been informed by a team of orthopedic specialists that I wouldn't be able to compete in my senior year basketball campaign.

My leg had been injured six games into my junior season. At that point in time, I was in a position to break the Academy scoring record. Seems amazingly trivial now, but let me assure you, back then it was a pretty big deal.

The fact that a group of military physicians were stamping out the most important thing in my life didn't seem fair. When the reality and the gravity of their decision sunk in . . . I lost control and started calling them a whole host of uncomplimentary names. I lamented their very existence and sarcastically questioned any institution that would see fit to bestow a medical degree on such obvious incompetents. Then, with tears in my eyes, I stormed outside, ticked off at the world.

Almost on cue a girl named Julie Nolan was moving up the street in my direct path. Julie was about 16 years old and her father was an engineering instructor at the Academy. She attended every home basketball game and was the closest thing we had to an avid fan. As our paths crossed, Julie could sense my pathetic state. Seeking to offer consolation, she said:

"Hey, Sam, what's wrong with you . . . you look like you just lost your best friend."

That line, coming from most people wouldn't have been significant . . . but coming from Julie, it quickly put a whole bunch of things into perspective. You see, Julie had been a normal 10 year old kid . . . until she got hit by a car one afternoon. That accident broke almost every bone in her body. She wound up submerged in a coma for approximately six months.

When she came out of it, she had <u>total</u> amnesia. Her parents had to teach her everything all over again.

She was just getting to the point where she could walk with a cane . . . when her doctors discovered she had a tumor. She wound up having her whole hip and leg removed the day after Christmas at age 14.

She had to endure painful daily treatments. Not only would she never break a scoring record . . . she'd never run . . . she'd never walk . . . she'd never even stand upright again.

So there sat Julie Nolan in her wheel chair legitimately concerned about my well being and my level of comfort . . . no need to expand on who was the winner and who was the loser in that little get-together.

Julie has since gone on and received her college degree from the University of Connecticut. She currently lives in her own apartment and actively participates in a variety of different handicapped groups.

I think about her often. It's too bad that people like Julie don't have more of a forum to actively demonstrate to the rest of us what winning really is. Pete Newell says it very succinctly:

"Winning is keeping things in perspective and maximizing your potential . . . whatever that potential may be."

Pete Newell

Pete Newell would really like Julie Nolan.

Process Vs. An Event

▼ Philosophical discussions about winning and losing are all well and good. You <u>should</u> keep outcome in perspective. You <u>shouldn't</u> get big headed about your victories. You <u>shouldn't</u> get too depressed about your losses. It's easy to write a book and <u>should</u> all over people. Reality, in many cases, is a much more difficult test.

Pick up a newspaper today and read through the "Business" and "People" sections. You'll be able to find documentation on three or four recent "losers" without any difficulty whatsoever. Here are a few examples that were public knowledge at the writing of this book:

A DISCOUNT AIRLINE TAKES A NOSE DIVE

Northeastern International Airways followed a flight path that has become familiar to discount carriers in the six years since deregulation: a too-steep ascent followed by a nose dive to bankruptcy. Starting with one plane and one route in 1982, the Florida-based carrier grew quickly into a coast-to-coast, 17-city airline with 1,500 employees. But increased competition and lagging passenger traffic forced Northeastern into court last week to seek protection from creditors, stranding hundreds of travelers.

Nearly a dozen small airlines have filed under Chapter 11 in the past year, including Air 1 and Air Florida. Under its restructuring plan, Northeastern is back to where it began, flying one route, from Ft. Lauderdale to Long Island — and still cutting fares: the trip is down from $99 to $69. That still won't lure some people, though. "I'm not giving this Mickey Mouse airline another penny," said stranded New Yorker Alice Rabinowitz last week. "I don't care how cheap it is."[42]

A TALL TEXAN GOES UNDER

Bankruptcies in the depressed Energy Belt are almost as common as ten-gallon hats, but the Texan who filed papers last week was no ordinary sad case: John Connally, 70, former Treasury Secretary, three-term Texas Governor and one time presidential candidate. Connally applied under Chapter 11 for personal bankruptcy protection and under Chapter 7 to liquidate the failed real estate business he owned with Partner Ben Barnes, a former Lieutenant Governor. Between them, they owe an estimated $170 million.

After failing to get the 1980 Republican presidential nomination, Connally went home to make a Texas-size fortune. Starting with about $10 million, he and Barnes built a real estate empire worth an estimated $300 million by 1983. But the oil bust sent the value of the partners' holdings into a free fall. Over the past year Connally tried to prop up the business by selling personal assets, including 126 prized Thoroughbreds and quarter horses that he reluctantly auctioned off for nearly $400,000.[43]

THE HUNTS FILE FOR BANKRUPTCY - AGAIN

Bankers who lent millions to Bunker, Herbert, and Lamar Hunt were shocked when three sugar subsidiaries of Hunt International Resources filed for protection from creditors under Chapter 11 last year (FORTUNE, April 1, 1985). The financiers did not understand why the brothers — whose combined net worth once hovered around $8 billion — couldn't somehow cover the subsidiaries' loans. But the Hunts' troubles were mounting. As the price of oil plummeted, the brothers fell behind on $773 million in loans owed by the family's Placid Oil. The Hunts wanted to reschedule. But their creditors, soured by the sugar default, demanded repayment. The Hunts sued 23 banks, charging deception, fraud, and breach of fiduciary responsibility. The banks countersued and sought to sell Placid assets, which include a share of the Hunts' Thanksgiving Tower. When a Dallas judge refused to halt the sales, the Hunts walked into bankruptcy court, seeking protection.

The brothers want to continue exploration, especially off Louisiana, hoping for a big strike. The bankers, however, want Placid money to be used for repaying debt, not for drilling ventures they regard as risky. Other parts of the Hunt empire are also vulnerable. Its drilling operation, Penrod, which gets about 35% of its business from Placid, owes some $700 million and is also behind in its payments.[44]

If you're struggling to make ends meet on a day-to-day basis, it's kind of difficult to get too teary eyed over the Hunt brothers' billion dollar bungles. By the same token, if Bunkie, Herb and Lamar are vulnerable to periodic failure, the rest of us should at least take note. Failure to some extent is inevitable. It's part of life . . . something to look back upon and describe as a "significant growth opportunity."

On the other hand, there's nothing enjoyable about finishing second if you've got the potential to finish first. Somehow you need to painstakingly prepare for success . . . and simultaneously develop the inner strength necessary to hold your head high in defeat.

K.C. Jones is pragmatic about failure:

"Losing is part of life. It's a part of life you have to learn to deal with . . . especially if you're involved in any kind of competition. I don't like to lose . . . I've never enjoyed coming up short and I will do anything I can do within the rules to win. By the same token, I don't let losses tear me up inside any more. I realize it's part of competing. That's just the way it is. In a weird sort of way, losing lets you look inside yourself to see who you really are . . . and to see who those people around you really are. Just about everyone offers you support when you're winning . . . it's those that offer me support when I'm losing that I consider true friends."

K.C. Jones

Of all the "coaches" interviewed for this project, Jerry West identified with failure the most. He was emotional in his description of the pain associated with losing and prophetic in his description of the role losing has played in shaping other events in his life.

"In my basketball career personally, I think I received every accolade or won almost every individual award you could win. But the greatest disappointments of my life, the greatest senses of failure I've experienced all came from team things. My summers as a basketball player were not very much fun. I can tell you, I felt like a failure because I wanted to win a championship so badly. I think maybe the only consolation I took from our team losses were some of the individual accolades. But from a team's standpoint, being called a choker . . . those things are real difficult to live with . . . and I don't think there's any question that they changed my life. They changed my life tremendously. I developed a complex where I felt that there were a certain element of people that simply loved to drag us down no matter how well we played or how much we had sacrificed. I think about those moments and I can still feel the pain. More than anything else, those years helped shape my life. They gave me perspective. They built within me an inner strength that has helped me tremendously in my second career as a manager."

Jerry West

Losing is nothing to aspire to . . . it's something to avoid. It's also something to put into perspective as quickly as possible after it happens. It's something to use to your benefit in preparation for the next encounter. Plain failure is one thing . . . failing in a forward direction is something entirely different. "Losing" is not the function of a single event . . . it's a function of your state of mind.

The important thing to garner from a loss is perspective. Individual outcomes do not separate winners from losers . . . a collection of outcomes over time make that separation inherently obvious. Winners find a way to grow from defeat. Wayne Embry says it about as well as it can be said when he recounts a season from his "Celtic Days":

"We played our hearts out that year and lost to the Philadelphia 76ers who went on to eventually win the championship. The thing that impressed me most about the Celtics during that period of time was the fact that there was no weeping. There was no sense of failure. We felt we gave it our best shot and did the very best we possibly could. That was kind of an awakening to me because I shared mixed emotions. On one hand I was unhappy because we lost . . . but on the other I was proud to be with a great team and a great organization. I realized that we had worked hard and came up short . . . and there was nothing to be ashamed of. So, we learned from our mistakes and the next year we went on to win the world championship and never looked back."

Wayne Embry

If At First You Do Succeed

▼ Learning how to put failure into perspective is a must. Learning how to put success into perspective is equally crucial. It's important to take time to enjoy the fruits of your labor. Whether that's a ticker tape parade down Main Street or participating in an impromptu party after a new prospect <u>finally</u> signs on the dotted line. Celebrating victories is also part of life.

However, there's an important distinction to make between "celebration" and "resting on your laurels." The world is dynamic. It never stops. If you want to continue your winning ways, you need to discipline yourself to get back to the grind. Success, quite simply, attracts competition.

You can readily identify true winners in defeat . . . they're the ones with their heads held high. You can also readily identify true winners after they've won . . . they're the ones deflecting all the praise while establishing a new series of goals and objectives.

In light of what he said a few pages ago about losing, this comment by Jerry West blew me away:

"You know, it was funny. I wanted to win a championship in the worst way throughout my entire career . . . and when we finally won it . . . it just wasn't that big of a deal. I mean I wasn't any different . . . it didn't change me or transform me or anything. The difference was in the way people perceived me. All of a sudden I was a different guy to them . . . it was kind of weird. "

Jerry West

■ Proven winners react in similar fashion in business settings. As Stephen Jobs, co-founder of Apple Computer, likes to say . . . "the journey is the reward," Consider the plight of Kevin Howe who is in the process of fulfilling the American dream:

Kevin Howe, president and CEO of Dallas-based Dac Software, Inc., launched a $50 small-business software program called Dac-Easy Accounting in April, 1985, and within a year his sales had soared to $3.7 million. Three influential computer journals declared his product one of the best of the year. He had a right to feel ecstatic.

But Howe was not. If anything, his sudden success had a sobering effect.

Before launching Dac with five other partners, Howe had been vice president of new product development at Taylor Publishing, a $60 million subsidiary of the Insilco Corporation. At Taylor, Howe had his share of winners and losers, all following a consistent pattern. "Every time I got overconfident about a new product, thinking this is a 'no-brainer,' I failed to do my homework," he says.

"Inevitably, that product never met our sales forecasts. However, when I was highly critical of a new venture, I thought the problem through backwards and forwards. That product always ended up exceeding our expectations."

>That lesson, says Howe, taught him the importance of "not falling in love with your success." So when Dac-Easy started climbing to the top of the software charts, his wariness kicked in. "I didn't let myself feel too good," he recalls. "I didn't want to start making mistakes."[45]

Kevin Howe, and people like him, continually position themselves for success. That's how they come to be recognized as consistent winners.

Being a winner is also a state of mind. It's a function of setting realistic goals for yourself that are geared to maximize your potential. It's a function of stretching to reach those goals when pressure from all around tells you to abandon them. It's a function of never letting a temporary disappointment obstruct the long-range view of your life.[46] It's a function of continually positioning yourself to have opportunities to win. It's also a function of critically evaluating those "positioning efforts." For example:

>*IF . . .*
>
>You haven't done extensive homework on your industry, your company and your profession on a regular basis . . .
>
>*THEN . . .*
>
>Don't bemoan the fact that you've been passed over for a promotion.

IF . . .

You haven't taken time over the years to really get to know your kids . . .

THEN . . .

Don't be shocked by the fact that you now feel uncomfortable around them.

IF . . .

You never make time to go to the driving range . . .

THEN . . .

Don't shake your head in disgust when your drives find their way into neighboring fairways.

Positioning yourself to "win" is rarely a fun and enjoyable experience. It usually boils down to extensive hard work, significant sacrifice and consistent execution.

- **Did you put in sufficient time in preparation?**

- **Did you execute your game plan?**

- **Did you play the game to the best of your ability?**

If the answer to those questions is an unqualified yes, you're a winner. This is true whether you're putting a ball through a basket, making a sales call, giving a presentation or trying to teach your kids to stay away from drugs.

Let's close this chapter with a wrap-up thought from Pete Newell:

"I think the mark of a successful team is consistency. I would imagine the mark of a good business organization is consistency. They're able to cope with the unforeseen things that happen. They may not always have the best players or the best product, but year in and year out they find a way to make positive things happen. They find a way to win . . . even when the scoreboard says they've lost."

Pete Newell

Enough said.

Scenario 2

(A peer offers a different opinion on a recent promotion.)

It does my heart good to see people like Freida make it to the top. I've known her forever . . . came into the company the same year. And with all the success that lady has experienced . . . with all the money she's made, and things she's in charge of . . . she still hasn't changed a bit. Still interested in what the people on the front line are thinking . . . what the customers are saying. She's one heck of an example of what this company really stands for.

▲ VISION ▲

CHAPTER 5

▲ V I S I O N ▲

Scenario 1

(A member of a promotion committee makes her opinion known about
the potential of a management candidate.)

*I think Jim's record speaks for itself. He's done his job as well
as anyone else we're considering, no questions about that. He's
an excellent employee and I hope he remains one with us for a long
time.*

*However, I question Jim's capacity for this promotion. Not
based on what he's already accomplished . . . but based on what we
will be expecting of him in the future. In comparison with the
other candidates, I think Jim lacks the creativity . . . the foresight
. . . the ability to deal periodically with gray instead of consistently with black and white. Jim is very good at "doing things
right". . . personally I feel uncomfortable putting him in a
position where he's responsible for determining "the right things
to do."*

▲ vi•sion:
   **to see the future; to imagine; to suppose; to
   form a mental image of something that is not
   present.**

Overview

▼ Vision, creativity and innovative capability are hot top-ics. More now than ever, managers are tasked with the "crystal ball" responsibility of predicting trends, making accurate assessments and manipulating the future.

This chapter investigates that responsibility. It starts out by distinguishing "Vision" from well articulated "Hind-sight." It then focuses on the differences between "Being Creative" and "Managing Creative People,"

Introduction

▼ I really miss Howard Cosell!! Not that Dan Dierdorff, Al Michaels and Frank Gifford of ABC's Monday Night Football crew put on a sub-par program . . . it's just that vintage Cosell commentary was something that was in a class by itself.

Consider a hypothetical Cosell barrage during a typical Monday night game a few years back:

Pre-Game
Comments: "While controversy surrounded the Jets' practice sessions this past week, one couldn't help but wonder if the bandaged knees of Joe Willie Namath can withstand the brutalizing defensive pressure of the "sack happy" Oakland Raiders. In this reporter's opinion, Broadway Joe has performed his last miracle, led his last charge, quite possibly completed his last pass. Frankly, I don't give the Jets any chance of winning this football game tonight . . . and folks, that's just telling it like it is."

Early First Quarter
Comments:

"Namath looked surprisingly good on that touchdown drive. The Oakland pass rush will wear him down before the night is over . . but if you're a Jets fan, you've got to be happy with an early 7-0 lead."

Mid Second Quarter
Comments:

"Namath continues to riddle the Oakland secondary! That last pass was thrown on a dead run between three helpless Raider defenders. John Madden will work out the Oakland kinks at half-time, I'm sure . . . but you simply have to be impressed with the gutsy display by the Jets thus far!"

Early Fourth Quarter
Comments:

"The Jets are really taking a giant step towards the playoffs tonight. It's just like we've been saying all along . . . never count out a team that has Joe Willie Namath calling the signals . . . that guy simply doesn't know the meaning of the word quit."

Post-Game
Comments: "The Jets travel to Miami next
                             week and that should be a class
                             match-up. They're shouting
                             "Super Bowl . . . Super Bowl" in
                             the Shea Stadium parking lot . . .
                             and who can blame them based
                             on what we've seen here to-
                             night."

By the end of the game, most of us had forgotten what
Howard <u>really</u> said prior to kick-off. We accepted at face
value his post-game analysis and shook our heads in amazement as he chronologically recreated it.

It was easy to get a real kick out of "the game within the
game." I got to the point of actually jotting down notes on
Howard's pre-game comments and then evaluating how
closely that articulated vision would match up with his post-
game analysis.

My informal research revealed that for the most part,
Howard's predictions came true. He did a thorough pre-
game analysis and everything pretty much went according to
plan during the game itself.

It was during the games where little or nothing went
according to plan that Cosell separated himself from the
pack. Subtly . . . smoothly . . . professionally, he could re-
position his pre-game comments and re-establish his credi-
bility regardless of the outcome. He was absolutely a master!!

Vision Vs. Hindsight

▼ Have you ever worked for somebody that tried to do a cheap imitation of Howard Cosell?? You know, the manager that points to the past as a means of entrenching their position in the present. Typically that manager will say things like:

- It's just like I've always said . . .

- If you'll remember, I predicted this trend long ago . . .

- I told you last quarter this kind of thing would happen, and now look . . .

A significant difference exists between creative visionary talent and aggressive manipulative hindsight. The former is the focal point of a world in a constant state of transition. The latter is a costly defense mechanism that can actually impede progress.

It's important to know the difference between the two. It's important because "vision" and "creativity" are front page news these days. They are characteristics that separate managers and coaches that "meet requirements" from those that set their own standards on a regular basis.

"If I could only find my way out of this damn forest."

Dr. Warren Bennis of the University of Southern California is a certified expert on "vision." Many credit him with identifying vision and creativity as distinguishable characteristics of leaders.

In his recently published book, "LEADERS: Strategies for Taking Charge," which was co-authored with Burt Nanus, Bennis defines vision in organizations as follows:

> "To choose a direction, a leader must first have developed a mental image of a possible and desirable future state of the organization. This image, which we call vision, may be as vague as a dream or as precise as a mission statement. The critical point is that vision articulates a view of a realistic, credible, attractive future for the organization, a condition that is better in some important ways than what now exists. In a phrase, a vision is a target that beckons."[47]

Dr. Harold J. Leavitt is equally credentialed in the behavioral science industry. He is currently the Walter Kenneth Kilpatrick professor of Organizational Behavior and Psychology at the Graduate School of Business at Stanford University. In his recent best selling treatise, "Corporate Pathfinders," he describes three basic types of individuals one might find in an organization:

- **IMPLEMENTERS**

- **PROBLEM SOLVERS**

- **PATHFINDERS**

Implementers get things done. They make things happen. They are responsible for changing the behavior of others around them.

Problem Solvers specialize in logic. They analyze, compute and reason. They plan, coordinate and "trouble-shoot." They make sure Implementers don't mess up their implementations.

Pathfinders, in Leavitt's words, "march to a different drummer." Implementing and problem solving may not be easy, but they're easily defined. Pathfinding, however, is a fuzzier piece of business. It involves coming up with the right questions rather than the right answers. It is not about figuring out the best way to get there from here, or even about making sure that we get there at all, but about pointing to where we ought to try to go.[48]

Embedded in the words of these guru's is the distinction between true foresight and well articulated hindsight. Vision is more than "running something up a flagpole and counting the number of salutes it receives." It's a calculated guess of the future, based on the cumulative experience of your past. It's the application of what you know, to the uncertainty associated with what you don't.

Vision is work. It requires effort. Successful entrepreneurial organizations treat vision as a duty. They are disciplined about it . . . work at it . . . practice it.[49]

One barometer indicating that "visionary skills" are alive and well in this day and age are the number of people starting companies in this country in comparison to similar cultures around the world. Based on a study conducted for INC. Magazine in July of 1987, Americans are two and a half times as likely to create jobs by starting a company as our allies in the United Kingdom. The successful entrepreneur seems to be revered in our culture. They are a symbol of innovation, imagination, freedom and courage.[50]

They are also invaluable. As pioneer psychologist Carl Jung observed, "the debt we owe to the play of the imagination is incalculable,"[51]

The role of vision and creativity for the modern day manager will only intensify in the future. Werner Erhard of Transformational Technologies, Inc., sees a day when managers will get paid for the future they create. To quote Mr. Erhard, "most managers spend their time attempting to predict the future accurately, the best managers are able to generate a future which was not going to happen otherwise."[52]

On Being Creative

▼ It will come as no great surprise that those interviewed for this book concurred with the academic experts quoted thus far. Vision is a critical characteristic of the successful coach or manager.

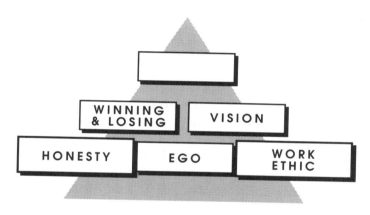

To have vision is critical whether you're developing a game plan for an upcoming opponent, or a sales strategy for a yet to be released product. Top notch managers find a way to see the future . . . then work backwards to fill in all the necessary steps to insure that desirable future takes place.

Here's what Pete Newell, Wayne Embry and Jerry West had to say about the importance of vision:

"It's always important to envision where it is you're going. Like in the game of basketball, I try to tell young coaches to always try to be ahead of the pack. Always aim over the pack. If you do that, at least you'll be with the pack. Never just be content to be status quo, because you'll be doing things three years later than they should have been done. You'll be that far behind. Try to envision the changes that conceivably could take place. You've got to be not only aware of the past, and certainly the present, but you've got to think of the future. If you don't do that . . . if you just think of the past and where you are today . . . you're going to be behind the pack. Visionary coaches are going to be ready for change . . . they're going to be tooled for it and by the time you adjust to it, they're almost ready for another transition. So, I think it's very, very important to know where you've been, where you are today, but even more importantly, where you're going tomorrow."

Pete Newell

"Vision is critical. You have to understand the obstacles that may face you and you have to be able to perceive the environment around you. To truly understand the components of that environment, you need to think about them <u>before</u> they are upon you."

Wayne Embry

"I think it's important every year that we add a new player to our team. That we create a new sense of who the Lakers are . . . every year! I don't care how successful we are, at least one player every year. And why? I think that an influx of new talent challenges the veteran players to play to levels they would have never thought possible otherwise."

Jerry West

Creativity, innovation and vision are often characteristics that are more easily discerned in others than in ourselves. I came across the following 10 item analysis developed by Craig R. Hickman and Michael A. Silva. Give it a go and total your individual responses.

WHAT'S YOUR CREATIVITY QUOTIENT?

Do you have the potential for executive brilliance? Take the following quiz to determine your creative strengths and weaknesses.

	ALWAYS	OFTEN	SELDOM	NEVER
1. You are stimulated by complex problems and situations that tax your thinking.	4	3	2	1
2. You dislike the sort of rigid problem solving that attacks every single problem with a similar, mechanical approach.	4	3	2	1
3. You encourage open discussion and disagreement among your people.	4	3	2	1
4. You read voraciously to expand your experience.	4	3	2	1
5. You entertain new ideas with enthusiasm rather than skepticism.	4	3	2	1

6. You ask numerous ques-
   tions, never worrying
   about whether they reveal
   your ignorance.   4   3   2   1

7. You look at things from
   a variety of viewpoints
   before making a decision. 4   3   2   1

8. You surround yourself
   with people who promote
   distinctly different points
   of view.   4   3   2   1

9. You make decisions that
   others call "innovative." 4   3   2   1

10. You search for new and
    better ways of approach-
    ing work within your
    organization.   4   3   2   1

According to Hickman and Silva, the higher your scores, the higher your existing creative abilities.[53]

● While it's true that creative, visionary people don't follow any set pattern or adhere to any "formula," they do exhibit distinguishing characteristics. For the most part they have a tendency to:

- **Initiate action and produce results**

- **Start the change process with themselves**

- **Find strategies that "work" . . . that can be implemented**

- **Tap the vision and underlying commitment of others in the organization**

- **Create support systems to assist in the analysis**

- **Look for openings for new possibilities.**[54]

Is vision a natural trait? Are you born with it? If you're currently not creative or visionary, can you develop creative characteristics? Yes . . . yes . . . and yes.

Some people are born with pathfinding, creative, visionary minds. The thought never occurred to them to do things a certain way simply because "that's the way they've always been done." They just naturally seem to ask the right questions and go on about answering them.

Vision and creativity are skills. As such, practice may not result in perfection, but it will certainly result in improvement. In many cases visionary skills are the product of your experience base. If that base is small . . . your creative potential will more than likely be limited. Consider the thoughts of Pete Newell and Claire Rothman:

"I think there's a certain rigidity when you start anything. I know when I was first coaching, I was very rigid. I was so involved with the way that I'd been taught and what I had learned that 'there was only one way to do things.' Basically, it was because I didn't know other ways, I thought mine was the only way to go about it. But as I grew, I realized that other people had different ways of doing things and you borrow from others. They borrow from you. That's how you grow. As a result, you become better qualified to predict the course of future events."

Pete Newell

"If your goals are clear . . . in many cases creative input becomes more focused. For instance, every day I ask myself . . . What's the best, most profitable path for 'The Forum.' What can I do to generate more revenue, additional events, cut costs, etc. If that's at the forefront of my mind, I find it easier to "hone in" on a vision . . . or dismiss it if it doesn't make sense."

Claire Rothman

If creativity is not a "natural talent" currently located in your "bag of tricks," it doesn't mean you'll <u>never</u> be able to offer useful visionary input. It simply means you need to discipline yourself to improve your skills in that arena.

Most of those interviewed for this project reflected on the development of their creative skills as a function of their experience. The more they did . . . the more they came to know . . . the more they knew . . . the more accurately they could predict the course of future events. Consider the comments of Pete Newell in an attempt to explain that developmental process:

> **"When you're young, there's a certain brashness to you. You just figure . . . 'I'm gonna make it no matter what.' There's so much you don't know . . . you really don't know what you don't know . . and that helps!**
>
> **I said in coaching, and I say this in all honesty, that the first year I coached was the first year I knew everything . . . and the last year I coached I realize how much I didn't know."**
>
> *Pete Newell*

On Managing Creativity

▼ <u>Being</u> creative is one thing . . . managing those <u>with</u> creativity is another. A few . . . very few . . . Fortune 500 companies are known for their ability to manage creativity. In the ultra conservative drug industry, Merck & Co. stands virtually alone in its encouragement of new product ideas and risk-taking. By keeping a constant interchange of ideas going between researchers and marketers, Merck has found a way to market one successful product after another over the years.[55]

Minnesota Mining & Manufacturing Co. also scores high among corporate leaders for long practicing what academics are just beginning to preach. Many research firms claim to endorse the rule that 15 percent of a researcher's time should be spent just "tinkering." But 3M has gone one step further and instituted it. Ever since the 1920's, when researcher Richard Drew surreptitiously developed masking tape, its first blockbuster product, the company has traditionally set aside one day a week for researchers to work on any projects that suit their fancy. "Even if a manager kills your pet project, you still have one day a week to prove him wrong," says Lester C. Krogh, 3M Vice President of Research. "And occasionally it happens."[56]

Managing the creative means inventing creative ways to manage. In the case of Hallmark Cards, Inc., it means some fairly "non-traditional" methods. Every Thursday afternoon at their Kansas City, Mo., headquarters, nearly 100 employees file into a small theater to watch cartoons. But not always cartoons. Sometimes it's Laurel & Hardy or the Three Stooges; occasionally it's film classics, depending on the projectionist's mood. And it's all on company time.

As members of Hallmark's 800-strong creative department, these writers and artists are actually doing their jobs — searching for ideas and visual scenes to use on cards, wrapping paper, and other products.

"Thursday Theatre," as it's called, is one of the tools Hallmark uses to motivate its most-talented employees — the people who give birth to the company's products. Indeed, without innovative concepts or eye-catching card designs, Hallmark would attract little attention on gift-shop shelves.

Besides showing movies, the company also regularly sends key employees across the country, even to other continents, with instructions to wander in art galleries, watch plays, or window-shop — hunting for ideas and trends that might translate into sales.

Sometimes it pays off handsomely. Several years ago, while viewing the King Tut exhibit at Washington's National Gallery of Art, one roving employee suddenly pictured the famous gold death mask as a puzzle for children. "That one trip has brought more than a $500,000 return," says Garry Glissmeyer, vice president of Hallmark's creative department.[57]

But what if you don't wield the power of a Merck, 3M or Hallmark? What if you're a manager in a company that's struggling to stay alive? What if you're a high school coach working for a school district that just had it's budget cut in half? How do you go about instituting creativity and rewarding visionary acumen under those circumstances?

No easy answers here . . . but first and foremost you have to take personal responsibility for establishing a climate that rewards creativity and innovative thought.

• CREATE A CONDUCIVE ENVIRONMENT

That doesn't mean you neglect bottom line requirements while all your employees sit around contemplating a better world. It simply means that you actively and visibly support the risks associated with coming up with new ideas.

That support usually takes the visible form of accepting failure. Realize that any time you tread on uncharted waters, the risk is greater than following a well outlined path. As a benchmark, consider additional thoughts from 3M Vice President of Research, Lester C. Krogh. "Probably 60% of the things we try don't work . . . but success at anything takes some gambling."[58]

Another guideline for the establishment of managing creative followers is to recognize the power of individuality.

• RECOGNIZE THE POWER OF INDIVIDUALITY

Come to grips with the fact that personal likes and dislikes have little to do with overall contribution. As K.C. Jones said during his interview:

"I have never not played a player because I didn't like him personally or because other members of the team didn't like him personally. Situations like those can be extremely uncomfortable . . . but you have to do what's best for the success of the franchise . . . regardless of personal preference."

K.C. Jones

Creative, forward thinking individuals can sometimes be difficult to get along with. As a manager, you need to show a keen appreciation of every follower's unique characteristics as they relate to your organization's objectives.[59] Welcome constructive conflict. Find a way to mold the visionary talents of your people with the non-negotiable day-to-day responsibilities of your work group. Admittedly, this task is much easier said than done, but it is a prerequisite for survival in today's competitive world. Leadership Style and the individual nature of its application will be discussed in detail in Chapter 8.

Finally, if you truly want to foster a creative climate in which your followers can flourish . . . stay out of their way.

• STAY OUT OF THEIR WAY

Creativity and vision are skills that can rarely be coerced.

In recent research, Teresa M. Amabile, an assistant professor of psychology at Brandeis University and an associate of the Center for Creative Leadership, interviewed 46 research and development managers in over two dozen companies to learn which factors stimulate creativity and which ones inhibit it.

"Freedom" was the most commonly mentioned environmental stimulant for creativity. According to Amabile, this meant "freedom in deciding what to do or how to do it, a sense of control over one's ideas, a freedom from having to meet someone else's constraints, a generally open atmosphere."[60]

Listen to Doug Collins describe how to "manage" a superstar.

"I think that a superstar, a Michael Jordan, a Magic Johnson, a Larry Bird . . . those guys are such winners that they help you coach the team every day by the way they come to work. It makes it easy when your best player sets the tone. My job is to create an environment for Michael to do his thing. We're going to live or die based on what he is able to create come game time. I know that . . . his teammates know that . . . and our opponents know that."

Doug Collins

A little of Michael, Magic and Larry is in all of us. We may not be able to dribble through traffic, rise above the rim and cradle dunk a leather ball while a capacity crowd ooohs and ahhhs in the stands . . . but we do possess creative potential . . . we do have experience . . . and we can be counted on to supply an accurate vision of the future.

Managers that can find a way to unleash that potential are the managers that are destined for extended success. It's as simple as that.

Scenario 2

(The promotion committee gets a different viewpoint on Jim's future.)

It's clear to me that Jim is the most qualified resource we have for this position. His creativity and ability to think on his feet have been demonstrated time and time again.

He has a focus on the future. He's always thinking through new and creative ways to cut costs without sacrificing quality. And, given all the change this place is going to experience over the next year or so, I think Jim would be a great fit.

▲ STYLE ▲

CHAPTER 6

▲ S T Y L E ▲

Scenario 1

(A frustrated employee shares his perception with a friend.)

You've heard of people that just sort of naturally do the right thing at the right time? My boss is just the opposite . . . somehow, some way he makes an absolute mess out of just about every management opportunity he gets. He talks when he should listen . . . delegates when he should direct . . . confronts when he should cooperate. I'm sure he means well, but I just don't know how much more of this I can stand.

▲ lead • er • ship style:
  The behavior patterns of the leader . . . as perceived by the follower.[61]

Overview

▼ Leadership style has been a popular topic for a number of years. Theories have been tested, models have been developed and programs have been marketed with the intent of providing an element of predictability to the dynamic of "face-to-face" interventions. With all that documentation readily available, you'll still find many more questions than answers when it comes down to workable, usable advice. This chapter offers a series of "how to" comments from the seven canvassed coaches in the following topic areas:

- **PERSONAL DEVELOPMENT**

- **ORGANIZATIONS**

- **POWER**

- **LISTENING**

- **CHANGE**

- **DELIVERING BAD NEWS**

- **DEALING WITH SUPERSTARS**

- **MOTIVATION**

- **LEADERSHIP STYLE**

Introduction

▼ The first five chapters of this book were offered as a framework for self evaluation. Subjective as the guidelines may be, if you:

- **ARE *HONEST* WITH THOSE YOU AT-TEMPT TO INFLUENCE**

- **DEVELOP A REALISTIC BUT DEMANDING *WORK ETHIC* (AND HOLD YOURSELF TO IT)**

- **KEEP YOUR *EGO* IN CHECK**

- **ACCURATELY DEFINE WHAT *"WINNING AND LOSING"* REALLY ARE**

- **AND MAKE A CONCERTED EFFORT TO EN-*VISION* THE COURSE OF FUTURE EVENTS,**

you will experience success as a coach or manager.

You may not "win every game" . . . but you will develop a base of power with your people that will position you for many more peaks than valleys.

With that base of power in place, the remaining question is one of face-to-face tactics. What do you say when the door is closed and a member of your team is staring you in the face in search of some answers? How do you deal with the employee that has all the talent in the world, but next to no commitment or sense of corporate purpose? How do you motivate? Delegate? Give direction? Build team unity? Discipline? In short, how about a little guidance when it comes to one-on-one, or one-on-team leadership style?

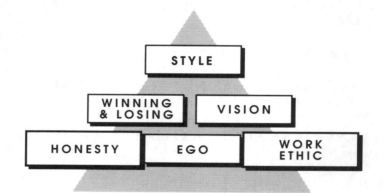

There are two things the interviewed coaches whole-heartedly agreed upon when the topic of "leadership style" was raised:

- *You must be consistent*

- *You must remain flexible.*

At first glance it would seem these characteristics don't even belong in the same book, let alone the same sentence. Consistency means rule books, regulations, policies and procedures. Flexibility means things like ordering a "Whopper" at Burger King, open door policies, participative management and followers "doing what they do best."

As those interviewed went on to explain, coaches need to exhibit characteristics of both consistency and flexibility when executing their day-to-day responsibility to influence.

Every team has to have rules . . . regulations . . . policies and procedures. It's equally important that the coach enforce the same in a logical and well thought out manner. Practices need to be well organized, start on time, end on time, and accomplish specific objectives.

By the same token, the truly successful coach is the coach that finds a way to respect the rights of each individual as well. In our society, everyone may be born equal . . . but that's about the last predictable dynamic you can count on when it comes to human behavior.

Some players respond well to public pressure from a coach . . . others don't. Some players have a natural sense of focus and drive . . . others don't. Some players bring a tremendous amount of natural God given talent to the feast . . . others don't. No "back of the book leadership principles" can be found when it comes to tactics. No fool proof "how to's." No sure-fire cures for talented followers that lack motivation . . . or motivated followers that lack talent. When it comes down to face-to-face tactics, the best advice anybody can offer is that . . . "it depends."

Typically, your tactics will depend on your:

- *Situation*

- *Followers*

- *Relationship with your boss*

- *Corporate culture*

- *Technical Expertise*

- *Confidence*

- *"Won-Loss Record"*

With those thoughts in mind, this chapter will offer a myriad of advice. No model to follow . . . no metaphor to translate . . . no matrix to decipher . . . just the topic by topic real world wisdom of seven people that can lead and manage with anyone in any industry. Their accomplishments speak for themselves. Their insight into the tactical issues associated with influence do likewise.

▲ PERSONAL DEVELOPMENT ▲

❝ *The only man I know that truly invented anything in basketball was Dr. James Naismith. The rest of us have been involved in an ongoing process of borrowing and refining technique ever since. That to me is the essence of personal development . . . learning as much as you can about what's already out there . . . molding it to meet your needs or career path . . . then sharing that with somebody else on down the line.* ❞

Pete Newell

❝ *I'll guarantee you that almost anybody that finds him/herself in a position of leadership today has been strongly influenced by somebody else. They've taken . . . I almost call it stolen . . . salient points from others and adopted those points to their own personality in order to be successful. Nobody makes it on their own and nobody should be afraid to admit that others have helped them significantly along the way either.* ❞

Jerry West

" Most of us get hired, drafted or recruited based on our potential . . . what we might be able to accomplish at some point in time in the future. Once you commit to a job or a team or a family, you start to develop your talents. Others begin to evaluate you on the basis of your actual performance . . . not your potential. I've always felt that it was up to each individual in question to take responsibility for that development. It may take a push or a shove somewhere along the way, but ultimately it's the people that take their growth personally that truly succeed. "

Pat Head Summitt

▲ ORGANIZATIONAL
PHILOSOPHY ▲

❝ Before I take any kind of job or get involved with any kind of organization, I want to make darn sure I know where I'm headed. If that isn't real clear upfront, it would be like starting a house without a plan. You build a foundation. You build one wall and then suddenly you decide that you'd like another wall a little bit higher and then you'd like a roof angle differently on the other side. It's not going to work. I think you have to have an accurate picture of what you're trying to accomplish before you even think about your tactics as a manager. And I think with the Lakers, maybe the one thing that I believe that has helped me more than anything else, is the fact that we know what we want in a particular player. We know what kind of team that we want to put on the floor because our fans and our owner have told us exactly what they want.❞

Jerry West

❝ Loyalty has always been high on my list when I think about my expectations of an organization. Loyalty up and loyalty down. I know in hiring an assistant coach, one of the first things I want to test for is if that person would stand beside me if things got tough. Not that I want a lot of "yes men" running around all over the place. We can agree to disagree on a specific point here or a specific point there. But I will always expect them to support our team and our philosophy no matter what. ❞

Pat Head Summitt

❝ Losing teams normally are not run very well. Their franchises are in disarray. There is disagreement on who should be traded for, who should be drafted, how much money should they pay, etc. One guy has a 'let's get rich quick' philosophy, the other guy says 'let's build slowly.' Still another says we have to 'do it now.' You have two or three philosophies in the air and you don't know which way you're going. You wind up just spinning your wheels. You keep turning players over and over and you never really have a chance to win because there's no stability. ❞

Doug Collins

❝ I remember something my father told me after I lost my first game as a college coach, ' . . . you don't take a donkey to the Kentucky Derby.' Translated . . . if you want a winning organization, you've got to surround yourself with winners.❞

Pat Head Summitt

▲ *POWER* ▲

" I don't think of myself as being on a power trip or wanting power in particular. I like to control in the sense that I like to feel that I put it all together and I make it happen. I enjoy that. I would miss that if I didn't have a position that had some control. I have a power base because my job is perceived as a powerful position. I recognize that if I say I represent the Forum, that there is some innate power that goes along with that. So, in that respect I see myself representing the power . . . but not being the power. I separate it. "

Claire Rothman

" I think there's power in practicing time tested fundamentals . . . whether it's coaching basketball, raising a family or starting a business. You work hard, develop a game plan, execute that game plan and critically evaluate your results. If you do that, you'll be successful. If you're successful, people give you power. But there's no easy way or 'cook book' approach to it. It takes personal dedication and sacrifice. "

Pete Newell

" *I think power comes from letting people know you really care about them. That there's much more to them than just being an athlete or an employee. That you as a coach are interested in them as a total person. People need to truly believe that you have their best interests in mind and not your selfish career enhancing motives.* "

Pat Head Summitt

" *I think another key element of power in this day and age is your ability as a coach to adopt and adjust to change. To keep up with the trends and the flow of events and predict the course of the future.* "

Pete Newell

▲ LISTENING ▲

❝ I try to find within others that spark that I can ignite and that they can ignite in me. I might be speaking with someone that's a tremendous runner in the Iron Man competition, and I could care less about that kind of thing. But maybe the thing that drives him is the same thing that drives me. So I'll try to find that common spark. In attempting to locate it, you know when you talk to me that you really have my attention. I'm really listening to you, I'm really sharing with you. I will tell you of my foibles and follies, and I'll make room for you to have them too. I truly believe that you are important in what you're contributing and you know it. As a result, you share information with me that you otherwise might not have, and I come away with something that I wouldn't have had if I hadn't known you. ❞

Claire Rothman

❝ People tell me I'm a good listener. I'm not really sure what that means, but I try to keep my mouth shut when others are talking and put myself in their position. Sometimes emotion gets in the way and I've got to discipline myself to concentrate on their message. For the most part, I just take an active interest in the people that are sharing their thoughts and do my best not to interrupt them. ❞

K.C. Jones

▲ *L I M I T A T I O N S* ▲

❝ *The current generation of women in the world of work has been educated for specifics. They might want to be lawyers, they might want to be accountants, they might want to be doctors . . . whatever . . . and we've said to them, 'you have the right not only to pursue your career, but also to pursue a full role as a woman, mother, homemaker, companion and helpmate to your spouse.' In doing so I think we create the 'superwoman' role. Not only do we give you the right to do this, but we tell you that it should be done with equanimity, with aplomb, with élan . . . and you start to think of yourself as never being tired, never being disgruntled or disappointed or less than a complete person. And that's simply impossible.* ❞

Claire Rothman

❝ *Right along with playing to your strengths is identifying your weaknesses as a manager. You've got to be objective about assessing what you can do naturally . . . and what you may need some help on. A lot of managers I've seen start thinking they can do most anything . . . deal with any kind of problem . . . and that's where they get into serious problems as far as I'm concerned.* ❞

K.C. Jones

▲ *CHANGE* ▲

❝ *You have to be flexible in your thinking. You have to be prepared to make changes. You need to be aware of the direction your industry is headed in . . . and if you allow yourself to become stereo-typed or rigid, the chances are you're never going to go beyond your current level because others will have passed you by. And how do you prepare for change?? By reading everything you can about your industry . . . asking yourself questions . . . asking others questions . . . going to clinics . . . fine tuning your skill . . . basically by working hard!* ❞

Pete Newell

❝ *I think that it's perfectly acceptable to say, 'I don't think I want to do this any more. I think I want to try something else.' I think that I have never been happier than in this third evolution of my life and I probably would not have made this change except out of my own desperate need and that's when changes are made. Somebody pushes you off the edge and says 'swim.' So you look at what you'd like to do and you say what do I have to give up to get there. If you really want it, you can do it.* ❞

Claire Rothman

▲ *DELIVERING BAD NEWS* ▲

&& *In situations like those I simply tell the person that we don't feel that he fits into what we're trying to do. I try to avoid telling a player that he's 'not good enough.' because that's rejection in a personal sense. He may not be what we want to fit into our plan, but I don't want that person to leave our organization thinking he's not 'good enough.' I may tell that person that you need to work on certain phases of the game and that perhaps if he can improve in various areas that he may very well fit in one day. I'd also try to go on and tell this person that if he were to apply what he's done up to that point, in his development in other areas of his life like going out into industry, into business, etc., that person will be very successful.* **&&**

Wayne Embry

" I wouldn't want anybody on my team that was satisfied sitting on the bench. I anticipate . . . almost plan for the disgruntled player to confront me about why he isn't getting more playing time or whatever. It gives me an opportunity to further communicate my goals and vision for the team as a team. When I talk about that person in particular I try to focus on their strengths and stay away from their weaknesses . . . on what they do . . . not what they can't do. I try to make them understand that their self worth or their identity is not wrapped up in the sport itself, but it's inside them. Secondly, any time I do give criticism or correct a mistake, I try to make them understand that it's the act or the behavior I'm upset with . . . not them as a person. "

Doug Collins

" There would never be a situation in my view . . . and I know that other coaches approach this differently . . . but I would never take a player out of a game knowingly after he had made a mistake. If he had missed a shot, even if he took a bad shot, whatever the mistake may be. I would try to time the substitution so that other things had happened that took away from the mistake itself. Often it's an embarrassment or a put-down when as soon as a mistake is made, bang, a substitute's up there and now the player comes out and you read him the riot act. I don't think that in all my years of coaching I ever met a player on the court and ever said anything derogatory to him. If I was upset, which many times I was, I wouldn't say much at all. Now, maybe at halftime, usually not after the game, but the next day at practice, you can almost bet that I would say something about it. But again, it's being conscious and being aware of over-flogging somebody by doing it in a public way that is going to put a person down or embarrass him . . . and that doesn't do anybody any good. "

Pete Newell

▲ DEALING WITH SUPERSTARS ▲

" *The trouble with a lot of people today is that too many of them were born on third base . . . and they've spent their whole life thinking they hit a triple. It's tough to bring those folks down to reality sometimes, but that's the communication challenge that faces most managers that deal with gifted followers. Personally, I think you've got to be real up front . . . and in some cases very directive with any player that thinks they're bigger than the system itself.* "

Pat Head Summitt

" *Superstars . . . true superstars . . . need leeway. Usually if you give them that leeway, they find a way to make the other players around them better.* "

Wayne Embry

" *I've always found that the true superstars are the people you have to be least concerned with because they are unbelievable in their mental approach to utilizing their talent. They find a way night in and night out to excel.* "

Doug Collins

❝ I think if there was a mark on my teams . . . you know, a way to identify them, I would say it would probably be the 'oneness' of the team. That even though we had different degrees of players, that there was a single standard of treatment. I felt as a coach that I should be more concerned with the treatment of the lowest man on my team than I was with the highest. In other words, the superstar, he was getting enough adulation, he was getting enough print, he was getting enough attention, and he was getting many, many benefits. The fellow that was at the end of my bench that worked very, very hard in practice, that wasn't endowed with the abilities of the super player or the star player, and yet he was out there in the practice sessions making it possible for our team to be successful . . . I was more interested in his feelings and I probably catered more to him because I respected so much that he was doing all this work without getting any of this adulation, without getting any of this print, without getting any of the real attention. That's just the way I felt. ❞

Pete Newell

❝ I think there has to be different rules for superstars. Do you treat them differently? . . . of course you do. You have to treat the situation as it needs to be treated because the true value of the superstar is the ability to elevate everyone around them a notch or two higher. . . and because they have the ability to do that . . . everyone around them benefits from the association. ❞

Claire Rothman

" *I don't want to treat a superstar differently. I think that you can impress upon that superstar the importance of the overall cause . . . working toward a common goal, and that goal is to win. I think that if you can communicate that to the superstar, he'll respect it. As he respects it . . . others are going to respect it. Then I think you have a chance of getting everybody working toward a common goal.* "

Wayne Embry

" *A lot of the people I coach have been put on a pedestal since they were 14 or 15 years old. Life has sort of revolved around their needs. It's tough to know what's reality and what isn't . . . they develop a jaded view of life itself. I think the most important thing you can do when dealing with people like these is to earn their trust . . . make them believe that you have the team's best interests in mind as well as their best interest in mind . . . and usually that bonding process takes quite a bit of time.* "

Doug Collins

▲ *MOTIVATION* ▲

❝ *Motivation is an individual thing. You've got to find out what makes each individual person tick. I will ask our players very early on . . . 'What motivates you? How do you get yourself going inside?' When they answer those questions, I listen very intently . . . because that's information that's very valuable to me.* ❞

Pat Head Summitt

❝ *I think motivation is directly related to mind set . . . a person in an ordinary frame of mind will do ordinary things . . . a person in an extra-ordinary frame of mind will do extra-ordinary things.* ❞

Jerry West

❝ *Motivation is commitment to a goal or a task . . . you've got to feel it . . . feel part of it. That doesn't come from one person . . . especially a coach. It comes from inside . . . it comes from that player's teammates . . . it comes from the organization itself.* ❞

K.C. Jones

" The thing that always motivated me the most was being part of a team . . . the unity and mutual respect we had for each other. When I was with the Celtics, Red Auerbach was a master at creating the environment where motivation could take place. He had the ability of making the 12th man feel as important as the superstar. He would come in and cite some minor thing that happened during the course of a game or in practice and would come up and give me a pat on the back. He would remember something that was very trite or very meaningless in my opinion, but he would remember it and he would say to me, 'Gee, that was a great pass you made' and I quite often wouldn't even remember the pass, but it made me feel important, it made me feel part of the team. "

Wayne Embry

" I think my personality is very strong. I'm very full of energy and I can charge people up around me by the way I walk and talk and by the excitement that I create. Conversely, if I have a down day, I spread it all over, so I have to be careful about that. "

Claire Rothman

❝ Motivation is nothing you do to someone . . . it's something you can allow to take place. You never want to restrict your people by inhibiting the wonderful gifts they have . . . it's like having an eight cylinder car and forcing it to run on four cylinders. Give people the opportunity to take full advantage of their talents . . . that will motivate them. ❞

Jerry West

❝ I want our guys to love what they're doing and I want them to appreciate it and I try to treat all of them a little differently because we're all different people. I might be able to motivate you by pressing you verbally and the other guy, your teammate, might not be able to deal with that, so I've got to deal with him in a different way. ❞

Doug Collins

❝ To motivate a player . . . I leave that to the player. I can do a little bit of it, but I can't go into every ballgame and have this big 'rah rah' speech going. That would make everybody sick after awhile. ❞

K.C. Jones

❝ When I ask you to reach back and to really pull from within, I'm right there . . . and I think that's very important. I'm not an isolated ivory tower person that comes in and says, 'OK, this is what you're going to do. Good-bye, let me know how it works out.' I'm really there, I'm hands on. If there's a problem, I'm right there. Sometimes I feel like a cheerleader. So I think part of the puzzle on motivation is involvement. But everyone has a different motivation system. How do you make the dog run around the track? You put the rabbit in front of him. I judge other people by myself. I don't like to be motivated that way. I don't like to have the carrot held in front of me. I like to feel that my ego is so big that I want to do the job really well, that my aim is always for perfection. So I don't work with the carrot principle, although that's a very effective principle. It doesn't work well for me. ❞

Claire Rothman

❝ To motivate is to know. I think you have to know that individual. You have to know the needs of that individual. You have to know how to appeal to that individual's emotions, that individual's ego, that individual's sense of belonging. He is a person, he is a human being. All people are not the same. We all have different problems and different needs. I think it's important to know a person and to understand a person before you can begin to motivate a person. ❞

Wayne Embry

‘‘ *I think it's very difficult to motivate people if you get too far from them. You've got to be there . . . close to them . . . know their problems . . . know their strengths.* ’’

Pete Newell

‘‘ *To me, people that work through intimidation are missing the boat. I would like to have the people that work for me not think of me as their boss. I think the atmosphere is much more relaxed and comfortable and people get much more accomplished that way.* ’’

Jerry West

▲ *LEADERSHIP STYLE* ▲

❝ *There's nothing conscious I do when it comes to leading others. I trust my instincts and stay focused on the objective of winning basketball games. I try to develop professional, trusting, open relationships with every member of our organization and just sort of let the rest of it fall into place.* ❞

K.C. Jones

❝ *I think if people do respond to my leadership style, it's because they can see I do my job well, because I am fair and because I expect no less of myself than I expect of them.* ❞

Claire Rothman

❝ *I guess I'd describe my style as one of always trying to communicate. I think through open, honest communication you can solve a lot of existing problems as well as prevent future ones from cropping up. One thing I would add on this . . . you earn the right to communicate every day with your people. They've got to see you . . . respect you . . . know that they can trust you . . . before they will ever openly communicate with you.* ❞

Wayne Embry

❝ Leaders to me are people that just sort of emerge from the pack. If you put 20 people in a room and just had them start talking, somebody would emerge and take charge of those 20 people. That's a little bit different than being put in a formal leadership role with a title like 'Coach' or 'Manager.' In those situations I've always felt it was a question of gaining your team's respect versus campaigning for popularity . . . I've always relied on instinct in those situations as opposed to following a well orchestrated game plan on how I was going to go about influencing somebody. ❞

Doug Collins

❝ People who are leaders are instinctive. I really believe that I'm instinctive with regards to people and that maybe is my best strength as a person working in management. ❞

Jerry West

" I would say that my style somewhat is to invest in each person's position, a level of importance, because it is important no matter how mundane it is. But I try to get that to the person doing it, to let him know how what he contributes or what he may neglect will effect the overall, and to show them that I have an appreciation because I'm the one sitting with the overview and I see how what they do fits in. I then tell them sincerely that I think they are the best expert for what it is they do. If they're running the parking lot, if they're the chief telephone operator, or if they're an assistant operator, or if they clean the restrooms. They really know what they do far better than I do. So, while I may have an overview of how it fits in and where it is on my importance scale at that time, they have the best expertise. So I listen for their input and I'm a benevolent dictator. I may not always take their advice, but I'll always consider it. It's always part of my consideration process. "

Claire Rothman

" I think that you always get tested as a coach. It's like your kids test you. You know, what they can get away with . . . what goes and what doesn't . . . they find out from day to day if you waiver in that. It's the same in coaching. For instance, if our team bus leaves at 5:00 . . . and 5:00 comes and Michael Jordan's not on the bus . . . if we leave to go call Michael to make sure he gets on the bus, then I better make sure that I do that every day for every player. If I don't do that . . . I'll lose these guys for sure. "

Doug Collins

❝ *All these guys are different. They've all been raised differently, they all have different backgrounds, they all want different things in life, but my job is to try to get them focused in on the one thing that we all want most and that's to win as a team. You try to take diverse people with diverse backgrounds and get them focusing in on that same goal. That's your challenge as a coach because a player thinks selfishly and that's the nature of it. You have an agent who represents the player who's telling them you must get your playing time, you must get your stats and all those things so you can make a lot of money. As a coach, you're saying you've got to make that extra pass or you've got to get that rebound or you've got to set that good screen so we can win. So he's getting torn. As a coach you're saying hey, if we win, we'll all be rewarded. You've got the agent saying, 'If you score 25, somebody out there's going to pay you a lot of money.' That's why you see some of these guys making a terrific amount of money who will always be losers . . . they're concerned with nothing but themselves.* ❞

Doug Collins

❝ *I can be very cold when I feel that what you're doing reflects ill on the overall goal or objective. When you do that, I won't give you much quarter. I think discipline is important. I think we all want to know how far can we go? Where are the edges of the crib? We look for that when we're a tiny little baby and we'll always look for that. I think that people that work for you still have that tendency.* ❞

Claire Rothman

❝ When it comes to style . . . I try my darndest never to make an emotional decision . . . and when we lose, typically there's a lot of emotion in the air. I'm paid to be objective. Sometimes the best plans you make never get implemented . . . sometimes the best trades that are made are the ones that aren't made. Objectivity is the key. ❞

Jerry West

Scenario 2

(A different employee shares a different perception of her manager's style.)

I don't have any idea how to describe Bruce's style . . . I never really even think about it. Sometimes he's very directive, sometimes he's real interested in my opinion . . . sometimes he just lets me do my own thing. One thing for sure . . . he's the best manager I've ever seen . . . always seems to know the right thing to do at the right time . . . I couldn't imagine working for anybody else.

▲ FOOTNOTE ▲ REFERENCES

▲ FOOTNOTE REFERENCES ▲

[1]"Where People Are Most Litigious," <u>U.S. News & World Report</u>, August 18, 1986, p. 9.

[2]"The Lawyer's Almanac," <u>1987 Annual Report of the Director</u>, December 30, 1987, p. 756.

[3]Ibid., p. 752.

[4]"1987 Membership Report," The American Bar Association, December, 1987, p. 163.

[5]Ibid., p. 163.

[6]Ibid., p. 163.

[7]Beth Brophy, "Where the Really Big Money Is," <u>U.S. News & World Report</u>, June 16, 1986, p. 49.

[8]"What it Costs To Win A $3 Lawsuit," <u>Money Magazine</u>, December, 1986.

[9]Mortimer B. Zuckman, "The National Lottery," <u>U.S. News & World Report</u>, January 27, 1986, p. 80.

[10]Robert T. Samuelson, "The Lawyering of America," <u>Newsweek</u>, March 10, 1986, p. 61.

[11]Walter Shapiro, "What's Wrong," <u>Time</u>, May 25, 1987, p. 14.

[12]Daniel Maltby, "The One Minute Ethicist," <u>Christianity Today</u>, February 19, 1983, p. 26.

[13]Marisa Manley, "How to Control Legal Costs," <u>Inc.</u>, April, 1987, p. 115.

[14]Ibid., p. 115.

[15]Carey W. English, "When Your Boss Pays for Your Lawyer," U.S. News & World Report, December 16, 1985, p. 68.

[16]Edward R. Court, "Liability Roulette," Nation's Business, November, 1987, p. 4.

[17]Infectious Disease Colloquium Conference, September, 1988.

[18]Jill Andresky, "Wall Street Law," Forbes, November 17, 1986, p. 78.

[19]Robert W. Goddard, "Are You An Ethical Manager," Personnel Journal, March, 1988, p. 38.

[20]Ibid., p. 39-41.

[21]Thomas W. Dunfee, "The case for Professional Norms of Business Ethics," American Business Law Journal, 1987, p. 387.

[22]"Boesky Sings, Money Talks," Money, December, 1987, p. 14.

[23]Abby Brown, "Is Ethics Good Business," Personnel Administrator, February, 1987, p. 67.

[24]Robert W. Goddard, "Are You An Ethical Manager," Personnel Journal, March, 1988, p. 39.

[25]David J. Cherrington, The Work Ethic (New York: Amacom, 1985), p. IIX.

[26]Ibid., p. 3.

[27]Ibid., p. 4.

[28]Ibid., p. 16.

[29]John Feinstein, A Season on the Brink (New York: Macmillan Publishing Company, 1986).

[30]Muriel Dobbins, "Is the Daily Grind Wearing You Down," U.S. News & World Report, March 24, 1986, p. 62.

[31]Janice M. Horowitz, "A Puzzling Toll at the Top," Time, August 3, 1987, p. 46.

[32]Abraham Maslow, Motivation and Personality (New York: Harper and Row, 1970).

[33]Frederick Herzberg, Work and the Nature of Man (New York: World Publishing, 1966).

[34]Bernard M. Bass, Leadership, Psychology and Organizational Behavior (N w York: Harper & Brothers, 1960).

[35]Peter Block, "Empowering Employees," Training & Development Journal, April, 1987, p. 36.

[36]Ibid., p. 35.

[37]Tom Peters and Nancy Austin, A Passion for Excellence (New York: Random House, 1985).

[38]Bernie Kohn, "Pep Talk", Finance, October 15, 1987, p. B11.

[39]Harvey MacKay, Swim With the Sharks (New York: Morrow Books, 1988).

[40]Muriel James and Dorothy Jongeward, Born to Win (Reading, Mass.: Addison-Wesley Publishing Company, 1973).

[41]Ibid., p. 5.

[42]"A Discount Airline Takes A Dive," Newsweek, November, 1987, p. 67.

[43]"A Tall Texan Goes Under," Time, March, 1988, p. 12.

[44]"The Hunts File for Bankruptcy Again," Fortune, September, 1986.

[45]Karen Berney, "If At First You Do Succeed," Nations Business, June, 1988, p. 15.

[46]Bobby Knight in a personal letter to Sam Shriver, June 22, 1977.

[47]Warren Bennis and Burt Nanus, <u>Leaders</u> (New York: Harper & Row, 1985).

[48]Harold J. Leavitt, "In Praise of Pathfinders," <u>Working Woman</u>, March, 1986, p. 23.

[49]Peter Drucker, "Innovation is in the Air," <u>Modern Office Technology</u>, March, 1986, p. 12.

[50]David L. Birch, "Yankee Doodle Dandy," <u>Inc.</u>, July, 1987, p. 33.

[51]"Solid Gains From Creativity," <u>Nation's Business</u>, June, 1985, p. 80.

[52]Perry Pascarella, "Create Breakthroughs in Performance," <u>Industry Week</u>, June 15, 1987, p. 52.

[53]Craig Hickman and Michael Silva, "How to Tap Your Creative Powers," <u>Working Woman</u>, September, 1985, p. 30.

[54]Perry Pascarella, "Organizational Trance," <u>Industry Week</u>, April 28, 1986, p. 54-57.

[55]Fred V. Guteri, "The Art of Managing Creativity," <u>Business Month</u>, October, 1987, p. 36.

[56]Ibid., p. 38.

[57]Mark L. Goldstein, "Managing the Gold Collar Worker," <u>Industry Week</u>, September 2, 1985, p. 33.

[58]Ibid., p. 36.

[59]Eugene Raudsepp, "Establishing A Creative Climate," <u>Training & Development Journal</u>, April, 1987, p. 50.

[60]Sharon Welton, "How to Spark New Ideas," <u>Nation's Business</u>, June, 1985, p. 18.

[61]Paul Hersey and Ken Blanchard, <u>Management of Organizational Behavior</u> (Englewood Cliffs, New Jersey: Prentice Hall, 1982).

▲ NOTES ▲

▲ NOTES ▲

▲ NOTES ▲

▲ NOTES ▲

▲ NOTES ▲

▲ ABOUT THE AUTHOR ▲

Sam Shriver is co-founder of Performance IMPACT, Inc., a management and sales training company located in Escondido, California. On a day-to-day basis, he is responsible for the design, delivery and analysis of programs geared to increase the "People Skills" of professionals in organizations such as Merck & Co., Goodyear Tire & Rubber, Procter & Gamble and Bally's Health & Tennis. He is known for his candid and humorous style in delivering theory to practitioners.

▲ ABOUT THE COMPANY▲

Performance IMPACT, Inc., with its main office in Escondido, California, was founded in 1987 to provide quality management and sales training to its customers at an affordable price. They have developed outstanding custom training programs for companies such as Merck, Sharp & Dohme, Ciba-Geigy, Wausau Insurance Companies and Scandinavian Health Spas to name a few. They also have a full line of "off-the-shelf" training programs, as well as a full range of speaking services. For more information, please contact:

Performance IMPACT, Inc.
1855 E. Valley Parkway, Suite 206
Escondido, CA 92027
(619) 747-8309